YOUR NET DETERMINES YOUR NET

SHORT-TERM RENTAL OPERATIONS FOR NET CASH FLOW

BY MATT BARTON

ACKNOWLEDGMENTS

If you work with and for great people, life isn't so bad. I would therefore like to give a special thanks to all the great property owners who we get to work for every day and who are brave enough to ride with us on this rollercoaster of a journey. A special thanks to my team at North Georgia Vacation Rentals, who have supported me in this project, kept me sane in the everyday grind, and talked me out of a lot of bad ideas; Alex Young for his attention to detail and maintaining order in this business over the years, Olivia Batchelor for being a workhorse and giving me back some much-needed bandwidth, and Sara Hockert for her short-term rental expertise and being my sounding board. Thanks to Christy Tapp for running an awesome cleaning crew every year and keeping our guests happy. A special thanks to my wife Amanda for sticking with me and holding down the fort with the kids when I'm unreasonably busy and take on too much.

PREFACE

Good things happen when you sit down and put pen to paper. Writing this book has helped me clarify our management philosophy as well as consolidate our team's strategies in a way that has helped me more than I'm sure it will help any reader. As someone who runs the day-to-day operations of short-term rentals, I thought I was aware of the vast details involved until I tried to put them on paper. As one who values brevity of words, I tried to keep this as concise as possible while hammering the important concepts and adding enough of the tips and tricks to give a practical advantage to anyone willing to do the work.

A brief outline of where we're going will save you time and let you skip anything irrelevant. I believe most of it will be beneficial to the majority of people already involved in the industry or those thinking about jumping in.

The first three chapters will discuss the pros and cons of getting into the business. If you jumped in already and are drowning and need some quick tips for improving, you may want to skip to chapter four. The lion's share of value for those currently setting up a home will probably come from chapter nine, the physical products chapter, which is by far the longest and most detailed. If you are just trying to determine if you can manage a property yourself or how to select a good property management company, check out Chapter 12. Most chapters can be read independently, so feel free to skip to the information that you are looking for, but overall, most will benefit from the entire book read in the order it is given.

Thanks to anyone who reads these words and finds value. Just remember that learning does nothing; it is the doer that gets stuff done. Learn as fast as you can, but don't forget to take massive action.

- Matt

Definitions of Abbreviations:

STR: Short-Term Rental

OTA: Online Travel Agencies, i.e., Airbnb, Vrbo, Booking.com

Vrbo: Short for Vacation Rentals By Owner, one of the largest OTAs and part of the Expedia Group

Legal Disclaimer

The publisher and the author do not make any guarantee or other promise as to any results that may be obtained from using the content of this book. This book is based on the opinion and experiences of the author, but it does not absolve the reader of any responsibility when making their own decisions. The reader should never make any investment decision without first consulting with their own financial advisor and conducting their own research and due diligence. The publisher and the author disclaim all liability in the event any information or recommendations contained in this book prove to be inaccurate, contain any omissions, or result in any financial or other losses.

TABLE OF CONTENTS

INTRODUCTION

YOUR NET DETERMINES YOUR NET

A young fisherman drags his net up onto his boat one last time, dumping his catch onto the floor of his little fishing rig. Exhausted, he grabs the oar and makes his way back to the dock, where he begins to sort his haul for the day. One bucket of keepers for the market, the rest of the junk going back into the sea. So much seaweed with today's haul, as well as some dead trash fish, is not even worth feeding that stray dog that has been occupying his doorstep. 90-pound haul, 82 pounds of which were trash. Eight pounds of fish for eight hours of work, and now to mend the nets.

For the next two hours, the young man mends his nets and prepares them for the next day. Feeling rough and down, he opts for the bar on the way home. Another fisherman at the bar gives him a nod as he settles down on the bar stool. "How was your haul today?" he asks the young fisherman.

"90-pound haul for the third straight day," the young man answers with a proud grin.

And so it goes with short-term rentals.

The stories are big, and the numbers are big. But if you are new to the game, are you having a hard time finding anyone's net numbers? If you are currently operating a short-term rental (STR), are you frustrated with the net outcome after all the work you put in?

Before we get in, let's establish what matters. If you don't agree with me on what matters, then don't waste your time reading the rest of the book. The net profit is what matters at the end of the day. That's it. Short-term rentals are for throwing off free cash flow, and it takes a lot of work and industry-specific knowledge to get them to do that year in and year out. It's not worth owning short-term rentals for appreciation; if you want to buy real estate for appreciation, go buy raw land.

There is so much hype in this industry, and bloated numbers float around there. Six-figure incomes on midsize residential properties. Even if we find it believable, what does that number include, and what are they walking away with? Are they including cleaning fees in it? Local and State Taxes? If they are, that number is nowhere close to accurate. Also, who is being honest about how much time they are spending on their short-term rental? Is that even trackable, and how do you account for that? How do you account for being on call 24 hours a day? Could you make that much money just working another part-time job?

Short-term rentals are more high-risk and high-reward than other asset classes within real estate, and without risk mitigation, your overhead is much more likely to eat you alive in a downturn than renting out apartments or single-family residences. You can create asymmetrical risk—return if you fish in the right spot, for the right fish, with the right net.

So, back to our illustration. Unless you want to be one of those fools in the bar who swallows it hook, line, and sinker when the young fisherman brags of the 90-pound haul, you will ignore anyone who boasts about 90k of gross revenue without disclosing net revenue. Focus on your net and where and how to fish, and the net income will take care of itself.

First, you must decide if this type of fishing is for you. Some people want to sit lazily on the dock, drink beer, and catch fish with a $19 pole from Walmart. There is nothing wrong with that, but that's just not what this type of business is. STR investing is hard work and proactive, more akin to constantly casting and mending heavy fishing nets.

This type of fishing has a different intensity level than most, and it requires a certain personality. It is not a passive investment; it is a business.

Next, you must determine your customer avatar (type of fish) and where to find this avatar (fishing territory). Then, and only then, will you start looking at nets (homes). Every amateur wants to start pestering real estate agents and start looking at homes before they have any clue about what they are doing or have the money to pull the trigger. First, determine who your avatar is, then where your avatar is, and then what net will be most effective. Keep in mind that your net is not just the house itself, but the design of the property, the setup of the property (durable furnishings), and carefully reduced expenses (lower utilities, maintenance, etc.). In a proper way, what you fish with and how you fish determines what ends up in your net, and what you end up with in your net determines what cash margin you net when you go to the fish market.

But before we get to designing the net and finding your fishing grounds, we will start with you, because if you aren't cut out for it, you shouldn't even start.

CHAPTER 1

IS IT FOR YOU?

This business might not be for you. Or it might be. Or it might be for you to own but not partake in the day-to-day grind. I hope this book will clarify that for you and will help teach the novice and tune up the experienced. You will not learn enough here to become a killer in the short-term rental space. You will need to do the work, put in the repetitions, and get at least a few hundred reservations under your belt if you want to master the STR space.

If you're smart, you don't care about me anymore than to assess if I know what I'm talking about or if you should just throw this book away and chalk it up to a sunk cost. I will try to keep my bio short and pertinent, so you can assess my viewpoint and take it all with a grain of salt. I know that an author's weight is in his gate, so I do want you to know that I walk the talk. Culturally, we would be better off if we stopped assigning weight to words from people who have done very little of what they are talking about. Here is me in a nutshell:

IS IT FOR YOU?

I started investing in real estate in 2011, when everything was beautifully affordable.

I opened my first STR in 2017.

I have been a licensed real estate agent since 2018.

I launched an STR property management company in 2020.

Currently, my company (North Georgia Vacation Rentals, LLC) manages a nice little portfolio of 25 mostly high-end cabins, of which I own two, for an average gross income of around $100,000 per month.

We operate in an increasingly competitive market, being in a popular drive to market from Atlanta.

At the time of this writing, I have been doing this for seven years, which I would consider neither a short amount of time nor a long amount of time, but I have done just enough transactions to identify some key patterns in booking trends and customer behavior. Currently, we are making about 1,400 reservations per year. My perspective is from a business and investment standpoint, and I also tend to be pretty knowledgeable about the physical aspects of the business, having done a good bit of remodeling and new construction. I know very little about social media, decor, and things of that nature, so don't expect a lot of information in that arena. Overall, we have been successful, and I have seen $100,000+ in net profit on a single property in a good year. I have also made significant mistakes, from hiring and keeping incompetent cleaners for too long to making some difficult-to-reverse mistakes in furniture choices during initial setups.

If you value your time, you should always be willing to pay for consolidated, accurate information. One reason I took the time to write this book is because I wasn't seeing that in a book on STRs.

Well, that's enough for me. On to STRs. First, I would like to throw out food for thought on whether you should even buy a short-term rental and if you should manage it yourself or hire a management company. We will get to the specifics of this in chapter twelve, but I want you to read the book with this in mind. This business is substantial for the right type of people and completely wrong for the wrong type of people. People hear stories of the hundreds of thousands of dollars in cash people are making and think they can jump into space and strike gold. It's like the gold rush rumors in 1848 that sent thousands out to California thinking they were going to be picking nuggets up off the ground. The 2021 craze that happened after the COVID lockdown was an anomaly, and there are a lot of fools snapping up properties only to discover fools gold doesn't cover their overhead. That being said, there is real money to be made in the long term if you have good business acumen, and I believe significantly more than multi-family, standard residential, or commercial real estate. This makes sense, as there is more risk, more work, and more industry-specific knowledge that you will need to master than the other real estate asset classes. A STR is more of a business than a passive investment, and it really can't be compared apples to apples with other real estate asset classes.

You can also make money running a STR off of rental arbitrage, wherein you rent a space from the owner and then list the property as a STR. I have two such homes under such a structure currently, but they are difficult to properly structure and can be difficult to find a situation where it makes sense for both parties. Most of the book will still be applicable if you decide to take this approach.

If you are wondering if you should buy a STR, first you need to honestly diagnose your personality type. You are probably not capable of that, so maybe you should ask that friend of yours whose mouth doesn't have a very good filter. STRs are best managed by people who are:

- Proactive and self-motivated.
- Are not overly controlling and can roll with the punches.
- Take a long-term view of success.
- Can excel at customer service and be patient with travelers.
- Don't mind responding to customer service needs at any time.
- Know a fair amount about the physical aspects of houses.
- Know a specific market.
- They don't want to know or really care about what is going on in their house as long as significant damage doesn't occur.

If you do not fit this profile very well, I would recommend being hands-off and hiring a management company, or not investing in STRs at all. There is a certain amount of bandwidth sucking that comes from managing a short-term rental, and as a property manager, that is a lot of what I get compensated for. This is also the reason I chose to expand my STR portfolio and start managing for others, because my thought process is that if I were already on call 24 hours a day, I might as well do it at a volume that makes financial sense. I personally don't think it makes sense to self-manage just one unit, unless, of course, it's a cash cow that will change your lifestyle, but a homerun like that is not to be expected for investors with entry-level experience and an entry-level budget. Don't begrudge an entry-level budget; be thankful if you don't have the cash to compound the initial mistakes that you will inevitably make. I didn't attempt the new construction of a STR until I had already been operating two of them, and I'm glad I waited until I had some experience under my belt, or I would have made more significant mistakes in the design of the home.

You must always be on call and always quickly respond to a guest if you want to get great reviews and continue to get high-dollar bookings. It doesn't matter if it is a guest that wants you to tell them what the Wi-Fi password is at 10:30 at night as you are falling asleep, even though it's posted in 56 different places in the house.

You will always be on duty, which means your brain will always be activated, and your RPM's may never fully drop to where you are idling. I run at about 2500 RPM's on rest mode anyway, but it kind of fits with my personality, so it isn't that big of a deal.

Emergency or holiday crises in the middle of the night are not common, but they do happen. These things make people quit. I know one owner who had to leave friends he was entertaining on Thanksgiving Day to go throw out some bad guests who were illegally hunting deer on his neighbor's private land. This is an atypical type of incident and very bad timing, but for him, it was the last straw and made him quit. It wasn't worth it to him to be at risk of that happening again.

There is some industry-specific knowledge that you will need to learn, but I'm not going to make it sound like you have to have a 120 IQ in order to be successful in this business. You do need to be able to develop a system for everything and stick to it. You do need to hustle, and you need to be a decent person. You also need to be able to carry on with life without the burden of something going on at your rental bothering you. There is never a problem. It's not always a big problem, but there is always something going on. It could be a guest that you are afraid may give you a bad review, and you are chewing on a way to mitigate that risk. There could be some needed maintenance that you haven't been able to find a contractor for, or some intermittent issue with an appliance that you can't solve and don't know whether or not it will spring up on the next guest. If things like that would bug you to the point where you wouldn't enjoy life, don't manage a STR.

You should be realistic in that there will be multiple things you don't like about owning and especially managing a STR. Possibly you are in a job that insulates you from having to do things that you don't like to do, but if you are a solo operator in the day-to-day grind of the short-term rental space, that will not be an option for you. For example, I hate taking verbal abuse from rude guests whose issues are self-inflicted due to a lack of intelligence, but I can't tell them what I really think without getting trashed in a review. I have to swallow my pride and maintain professionalism, which is harder than you might think if you haven't had to do it. I hate being asked for information from guests that they can Google themselves, like the distance to a certain venue, once they already have the rental address. These are just examples. Maybe you hate calling contractors and trying to schedule appointments in a tight window or negotiating contractor rates. Whatever it is, just know that there will be things you don't like, so get over it or don't get in the business.

If you want to self-manage, and especially if you want to do it from afar, you will need to be on top of things and commit to the following:

- Don't buy the wrong property.
- Putting in the work to find good people (cleaners, handymen, etc.) and pay them well enough to retain them. If you are a cheapskate, you compound your own trouble.
- Put in the time to research to learn the industry (YouTube, online groups, podcasts, and books).
- Be quick to pivot and improve when things aren't going as planned.
- Figure out pricing and management software that works for your needs.
- Set the property up right with good-quality materials without paying too much.
- Figure out a strategy upfront for all the routine work, such as a way to resupply the

property with consumables without paying too much.

- Develop a system for everything. Maintain your systems, and let your systems maintain you. There are just too many balls to juggle in the STR space to operate from memory.

Before beginning this process, it's important to take a moment and reflect on your reason for getting into this space. Since I manage all types of owners, I've been able to classify them based on their mindset. The majority of short-term rental owners fall into one of two classes: they are either primarily investors or primarily second homeowners. Some people, like myself, are only in it for an investment. I don't use my cabins at all for family getaways or time off; all I use the rentals for is a vehicle to generate cash and build wealth.

It's pretty common for people to purchase a home with their family vacation as a significant consideration or to purchase a home that they plan to retire in one day, in which case they are what I would classify as primarily second-home buyers. This is not a bad strategy, nor is there anything wrong with that; you just have to know where you are on the spectrum. I have a lot of owners I manage, which are about 70% second home owners and 30% investors. If you are telling yourself going into the buying process that it's just an investment, let it be just an investment and stop caring about your personal opinion on the style of home. If it's your second home, then be honest with yourself that your choices are not necessarily going to be the best for cash flow, and your net cash flow is not going to compare with somebody who designs and operates their STR strictly for business. If being able to vacation for "free" in your favorite spot once or twice a year is one of the main reasons for buying, make sure you do the math and see how much that "free" vacation could cost you if things don't go as planned. Maybe you should just go buy a timeshare; I hear they are great investments.

If you are primarily an investor, then you need to focus even more on getting a winner on the first home, or you may not have the financial capacity or the motivation to scale to the next one. I did well on my first one, which gave me the finances and gumption for the second; I did well on my second, which gave me the capacity to build my third. I had to keep investing in that positive cash flow so as not to pay taxes on it! For years, I rolled the positive cash flow from one property into remodeling or furnishing a home bought, built, or leased. A loser will stall you out, but winning breeds winning. I have seen this in other investors I manage as well; the ones that did well in their first year expanded their portfolio, but the ones who didn't. You need to begin with the end in mind; if you want to be in it for the long haul, control all the controllables that give you the best odds for success right off the bat.

THE CAPTAIN, THE SHIP, AND THE SEA

To wrap up the first chapter, let me introduce another illustration that I hope will be helpful heading into the rest of the book. I have theorized that when it comes to short-term rentals, the success of a rental depends on three major factors, which are roughly equally weighted. About one-third of the success depends on the property itself, about one-third depends on the host or property manager, and about a third depends on the market. You cannot have sustained success without being at the top of all three of these categories.

To illustrate this, picture a ship at sea. Whether or not a ship stays on course and reaches its destination depends not only on the weather but also on the ship itself and on the captain. Your property is your ship, your vessel. If your property is subpar and not well maintained, you will underperform. If you are a clueless captain or you hire a captain who doesn't run a tight ship, your investment will underperform. And the one that nobody wants to think about, the sea—well, let's just say if a hurricane strikes, you're not going to land where you were hoping to. The sea has a mind of its own, and so does the short-term rental market. It has inherent and significant risks, and it does not have the stability or predictability of the long-term rental market.

Are these three things of exactly equal importance? No, of course not. The most important factor is, most likely, the sea. And yet, all three play-off of each other in a very holistic way. If the sea is rocky, the winds are blowing, and ships are crashing on the rocks all around you, that is when an expert captain might be the difference between being on one ship to survive the storm and the myriad of ones that end up at the bottom of the sea. Maybe your captain knows how to pivot on their marketing, their cancellation policies, or their amenities or offerings to stay competitive in a changing market.

And choosing a vessel that is durable—one that might not go quite as fast in good weather but is battle-proven and tested—may fare better in a storm as well. Some properties are built for bull markets and roaring economies; others are built for steady revenue and are not affected quite as much by the storm.

Final warning before I close the introduction. Don't do this business for the wrong reason. Don't do it because you are a little bored with your life and it seems like a cool new thing. Don't do it because you are chasing the wrong numbers (I want to own 10 doors by the time I'm 40, so I've got to pull the trigger on something). Go into it with a plan to last, with the intention to weather any storm, or don't go into it at all. There's plenty of people burning out in this industry, and you don't need to be one of the ones with a handful of fools gold when the tide turns.

CHAPTER 2

ACTUALLY BUILD A BETTER MOUSETRAP

I'm not sure if you have noticed, but it seems that as a culture, we are increasingly focusing on marketing and sales and less and less on quality. For example, there is no shortage of books on Amazon about short-term rentals, the vast majority of which are basic, shallow, and redundant, yet all the book covers and titles are quite intriguing. Perhaps if people would give content the same attention as marketing, then things would market themselves. My goal is to give you your money's worth by the end of chapter three, and you can have the following ten chapters for free.

One reason it is so hard to attract attention is because of the low barrier to entry in so many industries now. Size and scale seem to receive attention and prestige, while consistent excellence receives less praise and attention. If you will but turn your capacity to actually building a superior product, actually stitching a better, tougher net, you will not have trouble catching your target fish in the long run. Unfortunately, launching a short-term rental has a relatively low barrier to entry, as many people without any money or experience perform rental arbitrage, leasing space and renting it out with hastily assembled Ikea furniture.

And such strategies are often temporarily successful. In some rare cases, excellent marketing and taking advantage of market tides are the only things you need for success. Such was the case for a while, 2021 through mid-2022, as post-COVID

travelers took flights from lockdown and wanted to see the world (especially drive-to markets). After a short stint of dropouts by owners who didn't have the reserves to cover even a couple months of overhead during the COVID lockdown, a whole slew of new investors started buying and slapping up "Airbnbs" to meet demand. There was cash in the streets, and any old short-term rental was a bucket to scoop it with.

Things have significantly cooled off since, leaving those who got in hastily (often at sky-high real estate prices) scratching their heads. They didn't take the time to actually build a better mousetrap, to actually assess what the top 10% of rentals actually have that makes them better, to assess the cost of those competitive advantages, and to make an informed decision to go in for the long haul. In

2021, you could use an air mattress in the master bedroom and throw it on Airbnb, and it would rent. Now only the top units have maintained their top ADR (average daily rate) and reasonable occupancy rates compared to the boom.

Most people have no idea how much more the top 10% of units make compared to the rest of the market (hint: it's not 10% more). Premium buyers are compelled to book the property because of the "rave reviews" received by the top units. The top units stay booked in the off-season when all the other units have near-zero income but still have the majority of associated overhead. The top units attract higher occupancy because, after the weekends are all booked, last-minute weekday travelers will take their pick of the highest-rated properties.

I would encourage all looking to invest to not expect to maintain a high ADR and occupancy level just because the market stays hot, but to create a product that can reasonably expect a solid and consistent annual return because they have produced an excellent product in a seasoned and stable short-term rental market.

ACTUALLY BUILD A BETTER MOUSETRAP

Actually, building a great product is a byproduct of a multitude of variables, the most important being time and experience.

TIME

Time will take significant time to find the right property, and significant time to modify and set up that property. The only shortcut for this is your framework for decision-making that you have already nailed down, so that you can quickly filter through properties and know what you are looking for. If you know you want a certain size and style of property in a specific location at a specific price point, then that will save you a lot of time in the search process. Don't be that tire kicker who just wants to talk about short-term rental investing and likes to go out and look at properties and waste real estate agents' time. You are either qualified to buy or not. You either know what you are looking for or you don't. If you want your real estate agent to give you priority and take you seriously, and you want to work with a top-notch real estate agent and not a clueless newbie, then be a serious and educated buyer. It is helpful to have more than one property profile that you are confident will be successful, so that you have expanded options and won't hesitate when you see it. For example, maybe your research shows the highest profitability in your market for buying a two-bedroom cabin at the $300–350k price point or a five-bedroom home at the $500–600k price point. Knowing these are the two targets you are looking for up front will allow you to filter out the majority of properties quickly and have the confidence to move more quickly on one of those types of properties since you have already done gross income projections. Do the work up front to minimize wasting your own time looking at properties that won't be successful. This is one reason I moved to new construction: I got sick of wasting my time. The listing would look great online, but then, when I put my eyes on it, I saw how much work needed to be done. The numbers didn't work, and it already had multiple competitive offers on it, and they had a best and highest deadline already set.

If you are buying, it will still take time, but you will waste less time if you take your time to learn and know what it is you want.

Once you purchase the property, time still plays a major role in getting things right. You should already have contractors lined up for everything you want done, and ideally, you want to be on their schedule before closing. You should already know what types of furniture are going in the house and have either a property manager or your own team assembled to run the operations. Whether you have a mortgage payment or not, you have fixed overhead that is associated with time, and every day that the property is not active and booked will hurt your net return. This is the stress that every property owner feels once the purchase takes place (and often likes to pass on that stress to their property manager), and the time and planning are best addressed prior to the purchase. Don't think you are going to order a hot tub and have it installed in a week. That's not the way the world works. If you organize your affairs or have a lower net return, it's your call.

Time has a direct relationship with cash. If you don't manage it and plan well, here is how it hurts the building of a better mousetrap.

- Overspending to rush a setup causes you to spend money that you should keep in reserve for when things inevitably go wrong, need repair, or if you make an error in the setup or need to pivot your strategy in order to be competitive (oh, shoot, we actually should have a hot tub or pool table).

- Being too slow in the setup can cause you to add thousands of dollars of non-improvement overheads (taxes, utilities, mortgage interest, etc.), which can cause you to lose your nerve about investing in the quality and amenities you need to be successful. Depending on the time of season you open, you could also miss the premium booking window during peak season and may have to lower your rates.

- Being too slow on offers because you haven't figured out what you want will make you miss the best properties. A decisive and aggressive offer on the right property can only be made by the buyer, who has put time into knowing what their target is. Maybe the property is actually worth more than their asking price, and you have to have the confidence to come in quickly and aggressively. Lowballing a bunch of properties is terrible. The best properties go to the best buyers, and it's impossible to build a substantial property from a property that's not great (apologies if I'm blowing your mind here).

EXPERIENCE

Experience is something you can partially buy. You don't need to know everything; you just need to hire someone who knows what you don't. Speed with minimal error is a function of experience. Every set-up I do is about 5% faster and better. If I wasn't at least twice as good as a rookie, that would make me an idiot.

As a property management company, we include in our commission the time it takes to advise our clients and will assist in coaching them to a successful setup. We will assess and inventory the house and provide the clients with a list of what to buy and what not to buy. We don't assemble furniture, make repairs, or paint the house for free, but charge a very reasonable hourly rate for anything that the owners voluntarily want to pass off. Possibly your property manager has someone who will do this for you, or you can find a local maintenance worker who can knock out a project list for you. Believe it or not, someone who has hung curtains a million times can probably do it faster and better than you. If you do any part of the setup process incorrectly, it will cost more time and money to have it corrected. We have corrected DIY projects more than once from homeowners trying to remodel, repair, or install things by themselves to save money. If you are doing it because you enjoy it, then great, but don't think you are saving yourself significant money unless you are very handy and have a low-paying job. Keep working your day job and making cash, and pay someone to get it done right and fast and get that property live and making money. Also, you can't take a tax write-off for your own labor on your property, so knock off about 30% or so of what you think you're saving once you pay your federal and state taxes.

Even if you're not the one running the day-to-day, it is helpful to know what is going on. You can shortcut your knowledge base by doing the following:

Listen to podcasts and read forums: There is a lot of information out there from the hundreds of thousands of DIY hosts. Some of it is good, and some of it is bad. If you have common sense, it will be helpful to read through and pick up on tips and rules of thumb. But beware of the retired person who has one property, very little experience, and likes to post on that Facebook group all the time about the very little that they know. Most people who are actually great hosts are too busy hosting to participate in forums. I skim through posts on the Facebook groups I am a part of, have picked up some useful tips, and have posted zero times. A lot of the people who post on forums are hosting, at least partially for the fun of it, are unsuccessful in generating cash, and do not have the investor's perspective on decision-making. A lot of the forums are pretty negative and there are a lot of complaints about guests, so they may give the impression that half the guests you host will be problems. Also, there are a lot of people who encourage you to refund more than you should, so take everything you read with a grain of salt and know that not everybody runs their business like a business.

Find the local expert and pick their brain: If you scroll through Vrbo or Airbnb and find a well-managed listing near where you are buying, contact the host and see if you can pay them for a bit of their time to ask them a few questions. You can also do this with a property management company, as people have done to me, but it is a bit deceptive to ask for the key benefit without being transparent about how you intend to self-manage. You have to start gathering local contacts, and the best way to do this is to find someone who already has a network of cleaners and handypersons that will educate you on the market and let you in on their inner circle. Your real estate agent may know some people in the industry, and this would be a significant question to ask before selecting a local real estate agent.

At the end of the day, in order to deliver a better product, you have to know the traveler and the physical attributes of real estate that actually hold up over time and deliver better results. You better know houses or have a property manager who does. You should be asking yourself questions like:

a) What type of flooring is best, and how long will each type last?
b) How do I design low-maintenance landscaping?
c) What type of roof lasts the longest, and how much does it cost to replace it?
d) What type of heating system is most cost-effective in this area?

There are a hundred and one practical reasons why a property produces or fails to produce a consistent positive cash flow in the long run. Here are some of the major categories you need to nail when it comes to building a better mousetrap. Consider this an introductory summary, as we will do a thorough analysis into most of them in the subsequent chapters. Most of these (I would think) are not specific to our market, and most are common sense, but you have to be in the game and do a couple thousand transactions to hone in on what matters and why.

a) **Avoid Fatal Flaws:** Not to be too negative, but the first thing is always to avoid fatal flaws in a property. If you have a killer property, you can survive having one or two flaws, but they will still hurt. If you don't have a killer property, just one or two flaws will sink you. Some flaws that are fatal to a short-term rental can be an aggressive neighbor who doesn't like short-term rentals, no cell phone service, no reliable internet service, limited or bad parking, bad access roads, or a neighbor with a barking dog. We have one property that has a bad access road and no cell phone service, but it still performs because it is a gorgeous, private sprawl on the river. Is management more difficult, and do we have to refund guests because of the road and cell phone issues? Yep, but because of the awesomeness of the property, it is still worth it.

b) **Choose a stable market:** Opening a STR in an unproven market is more risky than you should want to. You want a market that has enough comparable properties and assures a reasonable level of success without being saturated. It is also very beneficial to have a backup plan for the home should the short-term rental market dry up or should you decide to pivot strategies but want to hold the property long-term. Our market is perfect for that, as we are a college town with a high demand for long-term rentals and a tourist destination, so if I needed to, I could rent my homes in the mid- or long-term market in about ten minutes flat. That's how good the demand is here for standard rentals. If you are in a market that is almost exclusively short-term rentals, you could be subject to an industry downturn that would leave you with no backup plan.

c) **Choose a good location:** What a "good" location is different for each market, but every property owner thinks they have a good location. I have had several sales meetings where the owner is quite proud;

they are only 25 minutes to You have to know what your clientele wants, how far it is from downtown, or the venue that your success hinges on. A lot of our traffic comes from wedding parties, and they seem to have about a 10-15 minute drive to their venue. If they inquire about a property that is five minutes away, they book nearly every time. If I tell them the venue is 20 minutes away, it's about a 20% conversion rate.

d) **Hooking amenities or unique features:** The only way not to get slaughtered in a competitive market or a downturn is to have some unique amenities or features that the majority of homes in your area do not. Our portfolio is large enough now to pick out the patterns and what makes a property unique. When things are slow, the 5-star homes with 5-star amenities get booked at lower prices, and the properties that do not have unique features don't get booked at all or get booked at such a low price with such difficult guests that you will wish they didn't book. Some examples of unique features include a million-dollar view, a full game room (not just a video game system), or a hot tub or pool.

e) **Sufficient Supplies:** You have to get used to the idea of overhead and not worry that it will break your bank. If your STR is successful, supplies will be a marginal cost of doing business. You need to provide trash bags, laundry detergent, dish and dishwasher soap, hand soap, individually wrapped bar soap, propane for the grill, and every other basic convenience that is reasonable. Some of this is market-specific; you don't need to provide way more than your competition, but you don't want to provide less either. Provide enough TP for the entire trip, but don't leave the entire case out. Some property management companies only put out a starter roll of TP or two or three trash bags, but I believe this appears cheap to the guest. Don't try to save a buck and make your guests go to Walmart to buy the basics. Travelers are paying for convenience when on vacation, and the top 10% of travelers will expect at least the basics when they arrive. Guests will often ask prior to checking in if you provide paper towels, coffee, or soap, and it's hard to recover and feel like a great and generous host after having to tell them you don't provide jack squat after they paid $1,200 to book your property.

f) **User experience:** An overall great user experience comes down to every step of the process with a guest, from when they inquire with a question and get a quick and friendly response to the cleanliness of the fridge when they go to put their groceries inside. Everything they touch needs to be clean and in good condition. Notice I said good condition, not top-of-the-line quality. In the physical products chapter, we will go over where we recommend you spend money and where you save, but what you have needs to be in good condition, even if it is not of premium quality. For example, we run five-star properties that have cheap Walmart towels, and we very rarely get complaints. But if those Walmart towels have frays and stains, then suddenly the property appears cheap and poorly managed, and it negatively affects the user experience.

g) **Marketing:** Better properties go a long way in marketing themselves, but you still need to have great photos, have them properly organized and labeled, and have a great listing. Marketing is not a set-it-and forget-it strategy. A good listing is tweaked at least a few times per year. You want to change your copy and photos as you get feedback from guests and see what they are actually enjoying about your property. You want to find ways to rework your copy to make it shorter and more clear so potential guests don't miss information. You want to list on new channels and adapt your policies on existing channels. Without proper exposure, you can't do the volume of transactions needed to make the positive cash flow needed to keep your property up to par.

h) **You:** The last major factor in building and maintaining a better mousetrap is you (assuming you will be the property manager). The manager is part of the product; it is part of the whole package that people are paying for. You must be good at problem solving, make few errors, and have good systems to keep running a tight ship. People are paying for the likelihood of having an enjoyable and problem-free experience. If you book a property with a 4.94 average and 250 reviews, you have a high level of certainty that there are likely not going to be any significant issues, and if there are, the host will take care of every issue that is within their control. You must be consistent in cranking out a five-star experience if you want your mousetrap to be known as a superior mousetrap. Your customer service, problem-solving skills, and damage control skills will be tested in order to keep the flywheel turning.

CHAPTER 3

THE METRICS THAT MATTER AND THE PLATFORMS THAT PERFORM

The metrics that matter in the short-term rental space are more or less common sense, so long as you don't get caught up in the industry jargon that people love to throw around. When it comes to terminology, people love to throw around things that they don't understand, and even if they do understand the terms, that doesn't mean they actually know how to execute them. Just because you can talk numbers and market trends does not mean you have the comprehension and ability to get those numbers. There are a lot of people who can pilot a virtual plane, but I would not want to land one I was riding.

The only metrics that matter at the end of the day are net numbers. All other numbers only matter in helping you achieve net numbers. Your net cash flow, cash on cash return, or net cash for time invested are the types of numbers that matter. Gross revenue, occupancy rates, average daily rate, length of stay, and all other metrics only assist your decision-making in trying to generate the highest net return.

It is very common for short-term rental owners to state their property's income, including the cleaning fee. The cleaning fee and taxes have to be removed from the gross numbers to even do a proper assessment. Cleaning fees for our rentals usually land in the $9,000 to $13,000 per year range, so they wildly inflate the property's income if they are lumped in with rent. Most DIY managers don't collect and remit sales tax, but if they do, that could inflate numbers to an outrageously inaccurate number. Our tax rate is 16% plus $5 per night, so obviously that jumps the top line "revenue" by a huge amount as well. The last thing to remove from the gross income line is damage reimbursement. Some damages will occur during the year, and if the property is well managed, the vast majority of the damages will be paid for by the damaging guests. Damage reimbursement should not be lumped in with income, as it dilutes the accuracy of how the rental is doing.

We will go into a few of the common terms and explain how they affect your bottom line. Your strategy for pricing and setting minimum stays is dependent on your risk tolerance and the amount of work that you want to put in.

Our rentals tend to have an average length of stay of about 2.6 nights, which is pretty consistent year over year. We do allow one-night stays at the last minute, usually seven to fourteen days out on the weekends if we have a vacancy, and at any time during the week once we have the weekends on either side of those weekdays already booked. In a strong market, we hold a three-night minimum on the weekends until about 60 days out and then drop it to a two-night minimum, but in a soft market, we allow two-night minimums on the weekends. Our basic strategy is to try to get weekends filled as far out as possible so that we have time to book the orphan days during the week and achieve an occupancy over 50% for the year. Length of stay is very dependent on the market you are in, so check what policies for minimum stay are typical and also what hosts are actually getting for length of stay.

Many hosts love to praise occupancy, but it's not all it's cracked up to be and has a direct impact on your bandwidth and overhead. Many high-occupancy properties, 80% or higher, could make nearly as much net income by raising their rates and having a lower occupancy rate but not having as much overhead. Very high occupancy rates cause a sharp increase in utilities, supplies, and wear and tear on all other directly related expenses. It also makes it difficult to schedule routine maintenance and execute on repairs and improvements.

Low occupancy is also a problem. Nothing good happens when a property sits unused. Even if you just have a ten- to fourteen-day gap between guests, you will have to stop by the property and make sure nothing is dusty, smells funny, or that there's no dead bugs on the floor. My ideal world would be three-night stays with a one-night gap in between year-round. Make sure you are planning all significant project work for the slow season and are utilizing that time wisely, not just catching your breath from the busy season.

Your daily rate should be in line with your competitors based on size, location, and amenities. You need not panic with a wide range of pricing, from your minimum to your maximum price; that is normal if you know what you are doing. Your maximum price for peak season should be at least 80 percent higher than your minimum, probably as much as 300 percent higher, if your market allows for that. What you end up with as your average daily rate (ADR) might surprise you. If you are marketing your property properly, you will be selling a lot of dates towards your minimum price, which will bring down your ADR. You might not have bragging rights, but if you keep your supplies and overhead at a reasonable level, you can still be profitable at the lower end of your price range. Never believe what a short-term owner tells you they are getting per night. I can almost guarantee you that they are telling you their maximum price that they only get on Christmas and Thanksgiving; they are not telling you their ADR, or they are only renting on weekends when the rate is high.

You need to be realistic about the market that you are buying into. At the time I am writing this book, we are experiencing low nightly rents, lower than normal occupancy rates, moderately high real estate prices, and high mortgage interest rates. It's hard for someone like me who won't lie to people to sell someone on a new property in today's market. I spoke a little while back to a potential investor who wanted to put as little cash down as possible and wanted to make tens of thousands in free cash flow while having us manage it for him.

THE METRICS THAT MATTER AND THE PLATFORMS THAT PERFORM

That's just not possible in today's market, and I'm not interested in working with people without realistic expectations.

That's not to say that the industry is dead or, necessarily, even in trouble. The short-term market is more volatile than any other class of real estate. If you are not okay with that, then don't play the game. I have one property that I built for under 350k that netted over 100k for several years in a row, and now I will be lucky to gross 100k. That's the nature of the bull I am riding, and I'm not going to switch to a different type just because the economy shifts temporarily. During the down years, you let the competition fall away while you hone your craft and continue to collect five-star reviews.

It is important to keep good records. You will not be able to assess the operations side of your business very well if everything is not organized and tracked. If you have good property management software, it will run income reports fairly easily, show how different channels are performing, and pull your income numbers quickly. However, to get an accurate report, you will likely have to adjust your rental income to see what your ADR is after commissions to OTAs.

THE METRICS THAT MATTER AND THE PLATFORMS THAT PERFORM

Booking.com charges 15%, and Vrbo charges 5% if you don't have the annual subscription, so you need to take that into consideration. You should be marking up your rates to adjust for these expenses, but they should be adjusted when determining what your place is actually renting for.

Managing your expenses takes a good bit more work, as short-term rentals generate a lot of transactions and receipts. Knowing how your occupancy affects your direct expenses is a needed piece of information when setting your minimum rates and long-stay discounts.

Calculate your supply expense by dividing your annual supply cost by the number of nights booked; just keep in mind that your first year or so won't be accurate because your initial supplies and backup supplies will be a non-typical one-time expense. Last year, our supply costs for our larger homes ran from about $4.17 to $6.18 per day occupied, with a total supply cost of between about $700 and $1,050 for the year. Our smaller homes (2 bedrooms) had a supply cost of about $3 per night occupied. These figures exclude hot tubs, whose expense per night for supplies ran between $54 and $1.98. We use a chlorine system, but the largest expense in terms of supplies is usually the hot tub filters.

Utility expenses per night booked are also pretty easy to calculate, but seasonality obviously makes a huge difference. If you are in a cold market, it may not be worth taking a low-dollar booking and having to heat a home at such a low cost. Adding a few orphan days when it's not too hot or cold outside adds almost nothing to your power bill, so if your other variable utilities, such as water and electricity, are not too expensive, it's not that much of a factor. Obviously, trash, internet, and utilities like that are usually fixed and don't enter into the equation.

Here is a list of the top known and recurring expenses I would recommend starting with when assessing a property, because if you aren't profitable after these expenses, you won't have any left over for capital expenditures. We will go into more detail on many of these later on.

- Property Management Fees (if applicable)
- Utilities
- Property Taxes
- Home Insurance/ STR liability insurance
- HOA fees
- Landscaping Expenses

- Supplies

Some properties have unique features that have an expected cost that you must dial in before moving forward. Examples of these are private roads with shared expenses or a long private driveway that will be only your expense; a pool that requires maintenance and expected replacement expenses (pool equipment, pool liner, etc.). When at all possible, get actual numbers before putting in an offer on a property, or at least before closing on a property. It is not hard to get an actual insurance quote; you just need to pick up the phone and do it. Putting a placeholder of $2,500 for insurance does not give you the accuracy needed to run your numbers correctly.

THE PLATFORMS THAT PERFORM

Choosing where to list your STR is not hard. If you want to do well, you need to be with all the major online travel agencies (OTAs). Currently, in most US markets, Airbnb is the largest player, followed by Expedia and Vrbo, followed by Booking.com. Some people find success achieving direct bookings through their own platform, but this is typically hard to do and a lot of work. We will cover each channel and highlight some key information, but they are all their own animals and take some getting used to.

AIRBNB

Airbnb is so popular right now that many people use it synonymously for short-term rentals. This is not a good industry trend, and it is to the host's advantage to have multiple OTAs with a balanced market share. Overall, Airbnb has a very user-friendly platform as far as it goes, with guests setting up and booking a listing and hosts setting up and managing their listings through the platform. That is where the user-friendly experience ends. Airbnb customer support can be very difficult to work with, especially when you don't know how to operate within the Airbnb system. The majority of their support is non-US-based, is often difficult to understand on the phone, and usually doesn't actually know what they are talking about. If you call in to Airbnb with a specific question, you will get a different answer depending on which customer service rep you talk to, and of course this is after getting every vaguely written help article sent to you to try to get you off the phone. As much as possible, we try to put in support tickets, as even as a Super Host, we have a difficult time getting to someone who can actually make things happen.

Airbnb caters to all types of units and travelers and likes to promote unique stays like glamping, tree houses, and caves. They tend to have a younger demographic and a broad appeal, and they allow for shared spaces. Airbnb is bent towards travelers, and they push hosts to have flexible cancellation policies and low prices. They make their money off of the travel fee (about 8–12% of the booking amount), and so they don't get paid if people aren't traveling. Hosts just get charged a transaction fee of about 3% for each booking. I would not recommend using their Smart Pricing tool or taking their rate recommendations; do your own research and use an independent pricing software (covered in Chapter 7) that will push the same rate across all channels.

Airbnb has some helpful features, like a local guidebook that you can share with your travelers, which is great for the guest experience and also reduces the customer service on the host as travelers often ask for local recommendations. Another great feature that they offer is a host guarantee, currently called "AirCover for Hosts," which is "3 million in coverage in the rare event your place or belongings are damaged by a guest during an Airbnb stay." They are good about following through on it and actually paying out legitimate claims, though it seems that they are now intentionally making the claims process difficult to reduce the number of claims they have to pay. If you do have damage occur, make sure you are as nice to the guest as possible, not only so they don't give you a bad review when you send them the bill for the damage, but so that you don't have to jump through all the hoops for a claim with Airbnb. The claim goes first to the guest, who usually declines it, in which case Airbnb will cover it if you can submit proper documentation. If it is a straightforward case like a broken lamp, a claim can be completed in just a couple of minutes, as you can just find a similar item on Amazon, upload the link, and submit the claim. Airbnb does depreciate the damaged item, so if you put in a claim for a $30 lamp that is 5 years old, you are not going to get $30, even though that's what it will cost to replace.

The tricky part comes in when the guest damages require labor to make the property right again, especially skilled labor to repair. Airbnb has many hoops to jump through for getting official quotes for repairing damaged property. This is all subject to change and probably will change, but the last claim we processed with Airbnb required us to get the tax register number, company name and logo on company letterhead, business license number, and every item on the quote to be itemized. On a day where you can hardly get contractors to answer the phone, try to get an understaffed and too busy vendor to promptly email you a quote with all of those necessary items on the quote. In a rural market like ours, many of the best repair folk are good old boys who are reasonably priced and great at their jobs, but there is no way you are ever going to get a detailed and professional quote like that out of them.

Another issue to be aware of with Airbnb is that they wield all the power to cancel reservations and refund guests. If their algorithm reviews a guest and takes a risk, they can cancel that guest at any point and give them a full refund.

Sometimes this occurs after the guest has been booked for weeks and you are unable to fill the dates after Airbnb cancels and refunds the guest. Airbnb is also very quick to refund guests for any issues or inconveniences on a trip. We have had guests get full refunds for a hot tub with some sediment in it after a heavy rain. We had guests make a mountain out of a molehill and get Airbnb to refund them entirely. You need to account for this variable when giving guests credit, as sometimes it is cheaper to give them a significant amount back for an issue, then have them request a full refund from Airbnb and get even more back.

When setting up your Airbnb profile, make sure you build it out with as much friendly information as possible so that potential guests can connect with you as a person. Airbnb excels at creating this human connection type of vibe, and many travelers are looking for a good local host who knows the area. Airbnb also has a unique co-host feature that is not available on other platforms, which is great for those who want to partner up with another individual to manage the listing.

Like all OTAs, Airbnb is clunky with pet fees and extra fees such as early and late checkout fees. I believe this is intentional, as they are trying to keep fees to a minimum to be more traveler-friendly and build their platform. Even if you have instant booking turned on, guests can send a booking request that requests early check-in but has no way to apply an early check-in fee. We will get to fees and early check-in requests in a later chapter, but it is unfortunate that there is no way to automate this. We send early check-in fees through the payment request portal. Airbnb calls the resolution center, and we also send the guest a link to the resolution center because many of them can't seem to find where to pay. The resolution center is also where we send requests for additional pet fees, since Airbnb does not have an option to collect multiple pet fees. You must disclose in your listing that there is a fee for a second or third pet and that you will send a payment request for this after booking. If you don't do this, your guest can and will bring three or four pets and pay one pet fee.

Even with all of its issues, Airbnb is the dominant platform in most markets, and if you are going to be lazy and only list on one platform, Airbnb would be the one to go with.

VRBO

Vrbo is the next largest player in the industry and is owned by Expedia. They tend to cater to higher-income travelers, especially those looking for longer stays in nicer vacation homes. They do not support listings in shared spaces like Airbnb.

Vrbo offers two options for hosts: either a 5% pay per booking commission or a steep annual subscription ($699 at the time of this writing). The larger homes we manage do between 21-36% of their revenue through Vrbo, so it makes sense for them to just pay the annual subscription. With our property management software (Hostaway), we are able to mark up rates for each channel, so we typically mark up the rate a little bit to offset the annual fee or markup the full 5% if the property is on a pay per booking plan. Vrbo also charges the travelers a fee in the same range as Airbnb, so they are making money on both ends.

Vrbo doesn't guarantee hosts against damage to their property, but they do have an option for making the guests choose between a refundable damage deposit for the limit you choose, or an insurance policy that they sell the guest. We also sell the same damage protection insurance plans through Generali Global Assistance, and they are good plans that do pay out in the event of a claim. However, a lot of travelers don't want to have to pay a damage deposit or pay for a $59+ insurance plan, so I believe this does hurt Vrbo in gaining traveler market share. They seem to be trying to operate at higher margins, between making money

THE METRICS THAT MATTER AND THE
PLATFORMS THAT PERFORM

off both guests and travelers and selling insurance plans, for which they get a healthy cut.

Overall, Vrbo is a solid company, and in our experience, they do have much better customer service than Airbnb. Vrbo seems to have mostly US-based customer support, though they do seem to be outsourcing more lately, and they are usually fairly knowledgeable and a little easier to work with.

Vrbo does experience a fairly high number of scammers, so be very cautious when contacted by any guests who are trying to contact you off the platform. It is usually pretty obvious that it is a scam, as the scammer always wants to pay off the platform and gives some excuse for this, such as their company paying for the trip.

Vrbo also has different guest review terms than Airbnb and allows guests to review your property for up to a year after they stay at your home. If you review the guest, it triggers a two-week period that they have to review you. Because of this, if you have had a good experience hosting the guest, it is generally best practice to request a review from the guest but not leave a review for them in order to give them as much time as possible to write a review. It's not likely that someone is going to leave a review after six months, but it is pretty common for people to be busy after a trip and not get around to it for 3–4 weeks.

BOOKING.COM

Booking.com has the largest market share in Europe but has a relatively small position in the United States. Its website is really designed for hotels and is clunky and not user-friendly at all. The information that the host uploads does not all get displayed to Booking.com guests, and the information that Booking.com decides to publish on the listing is awkward and insufficient. Booking.com gives you virtually no control over what your listing looks like, and there is no way to change how your information is displayed.

There is no fee for listing on Booking.com, but they charge a 15% commission to hosts, so you have to raise your rates compared to the other OTAs.

Payment processing is often an issue with Booking.com, with guests having more options to cancel or not paying until very close to their stay and being able to cancel for free. There are rumors that they are about to invest heavily to grow their short-term rental market in the United States and fix a lot of the platform issues,

but so far there have been no improvements. If you can achieve a certain number of bookings and reviews (that booking.com does not specify), then your account gets a higher level of verification and you can require better payment terms from the guest; until that point, you are usually riding the struggle bus.

Booking.com has a review score out of 10, which tends to lead to lower reviews.

There is no two-way review system with Booking.com, so you don't know anything about the guest going into the reservation and do not get a chance to review the guest. You can only respond to a Booking.com review if they write something about their stay; if they only give you a review score, you don't have the opportunity to do anything.

Booking.com guests are typically lower quality than Airbnb and Vrbo, and unfortunately, because they can't be reviewed, you have nothing to hold over their heads, which can lead them to ask for refunds and leave bad reviews without consequence.

THE METRICS THAT MATTER AND THE PLATFORMS THAT PERFORM

Getting a hold of Booking.com guests can be difficult, as you get a custom Booking.com email address, and most of the time the guests won't answer their phone if you call them. For some reason, they often can't find check-in instructions on Booking.com, and to make matters worse, Booking.com sends them a random 4-digit PIN that you can't see, which implies that is their door code. Our automated message to them after their reservations tells them to ignore this code, but a lot of guests never get that message.

Most Booking.com guests are as frustrated with the platform as we are, and we have been told by several guests who call us that they will never use Booking.com again.

Right now, we do about ten percent of our reservations through Booking.com. Most hosts in our area do not use Booking.com, which is why we do and get a significant number of bookings from them. Unless they make some significant course corrections, I wouldn't be surprised if Booking.com loses significant market share in the short-term rental space, as they have frustrated both hosts and guests.

Unless your PMS (Property Management Software) can connect to Booking.com and automatically markup your pricing and manage your listing, you should consider if it is worth the time, effort, and risk to list on Booking.com.

DIRECT BOOKINGS

A lot of hosts in the past few years have attempted to increase direct bookings, especially with the control flexed by Airbnb in its reversal of its cancellation policy in the COVID meltdown. There is always platform risk when receiving guests from another platform, from chargebacks to missed payments to Airbnb canceling a booking and not paying out because the guest did not verify their account. Taking direct bookings comes with a different kind of risk, which we will get to in a moment.

The simplest way to have a direct booking website is to just create a website for your property and redirect potential guests to Airbnb or Vrbo to book. This is very easy to do, but also accomplishes next to nothing because your website will be so small and insignificant that of the 13 people a year that go to your website, one will follow the link to Airbnb and book your property, which they probably would have booked for those dates anyway on Airbnb. This type of process makes no sense to me unless you are seeking brand recognition and have multiple properties that you are trying to promote. Most DIY managers with their own websites do not keep their pages up to date and functional, which has a negative effect on marketing. If one of the few people a year that actually stumbles onto your website finds broken links, dated pictures, and information, they will be less likely to book your property through any channel.

The other way to do direct booking websites is to actually have a booking engine on your website and take direct bookings, not redirect them to book elsewhere. This makes more sense, as travelers may be incentivized to book with you directly because you don't have a booking fee like Airbnb or Vrbo, unless you choose to create a booking fee. Many PMS have a website-building component to them, making this a lot easier.

There are risks that come with this, though, and you will have to become the payment processor, figure out damage deposits, rental agreements, and house rules, and remit sales tax. Airbnb and Vrbo remit sales tax on your behalf if you are not the payment processor, but once you step into that role, there are a lot more complications. Also, you will not have the benefit of Airbnb's or Vrbo's additional liability coverage or host guarantee if something goes wrong, so you will want to make sure that you have adequate short-term rental insurance.

If you have multiple properties, it may make sense to go for your own website and take direct bookings, but you must at least generate enough traffic to it to cover your time and overhead for the website and that can be difficult to do. SEO (search engine optimization) is very competitive in the STR space, as everyone from OTA and national property management companies (Vacasa, Evolve) runs paid ads on search engines.

One freebie that you may be able to do that will help will be to advertise your listing on your city or county's information site. Many local chambers of commerce will offer listings to all local hosts on their website, even if you are not a chamber member. We are fortunate to have a very active government website. Last year, our little town's website (Dahlonega.org) brought in 2.6 million visitors. If you do not have a direct booking website, you can just redirect traffic from your profile on the Chamber of Commerce site to your page on Airbnb. Every year, our direct booking site, northgeorgiavacationrentals.net, gains a little bit more traction and increased conversions on direct bookings. We are currently up to about 14% of our reservations coming through our website, which is a huge win for us. Just beware that by putting your contact information out there on a direct booking website, you will get phone calls from potential travelers, and in our experience, the conversion rate on phone sales is pretty low and takes up a lot of time. Sometimes you get a traveler that wants to know all about all of your properties, and you can spend 30-45 minutes on a call with the bride-to-be's mother answering a myriad of questions, knowing that there is only a 15% chance she will book anything, and if she does, she will be a lot of work during her stay as well. If you do enough direct bookings, just like with any other channel, you will get the feel for who will be good guests, who will be troubling guests, and who are just tire kickers.

Social media is another aspect of direct marketing, but it still has the same dilemma as a website: if you redirect guests attention to your website where they can book, you can make a little extra money and have more control over the booking process, but if you have to redirect them to Airbnb or Vrbo to book, it's likely not helping all that much.

THE METRICS THAT MATTER AND THE PLATFORMS THAT PERFORM

Social media done well is very time-consuming; unless you happen to be already experienced in that space, it may not make sense to invest a lot of time there. I fully understand that my opinion here is not accepted by many who love to champion Instagram and Facebook leads. The value I assign to social media is also subject to change should the market change, and anything I write here could be completely wrong in a few years. I do understand that social media is a huge driver in some industries and possibly in some vacation rental markets, but I would not spend a lot of time on it before asking someone who is "successful" at it how many bookings they got directly from their social media campaign. I have seen thousands of followers on Instagram for one single property, and that property had a near-empty calendar. There are exceptions to this, and some properties are so unique and social media trendy that they can actually generate convertible leads on social media, but not most homes. Remember that followers and likes do not have a direct correlation to cash. At some point, you will get approached by an influencer with a large following who wants to stay in your place for free in exchange for a promotion, but unless they can prove that they have gotten bookings and you can verify that with the other host, I would pass.

It is always good to occasionally post your property on social media, if only so that your friends and extended family are aware that you have a STR in case they ever want to use it for travel or vacation. Friends and family direct bookings can be a safe way to boost occupancy, just set expectations and don't feel obligated to give away your space for free.

PROPERTY MANAGEMENT SOFTWARE

Your property management software (PMS) is an invaluable tool if you are managing more than one property or are trying to reduce the amount of time spent on management. If you are a host with one property who is doing it for a hobby, you can probably get away without one, especially if saving time is not of great importance to you. A PMS properly used will help you reduce errors, such as forgetting to send check-in instructions, and will also update multiple platforms at once, such as syncing pricing across all channels. There are dozens of PMS out there, without any clear market leader. Some of the most popular that are worth looking into include:

- Guesty
- Hostaway
- Escapia
- Logify
- Beyond
- Hospitable
- OwnerRez
- Hostify
- Hosthub

We use Hostaway, and some of the features we find most valuable are in our PMS are:

Calendar Syncing and Connection to Pricing Software: Syncing calendars is easy these days, and even if you are using Airbnb and Vrbo without a channel manager, you can sync the calendars so you don't get double booked. What you need to look for is pricing software in conjunction with your PMS so that you can ensure they are compatible.

Centralized Messaging and Automated Emails: Automated messages are key to timely and consistent information flow. Do not use them to respond to inquiries. I have seen even amateur hosts use them as an automated response on Airbnb to let the traveler know they will respond to them as soon as possible. To me, this scream that there is no one on duty 24 hours a day, and if you have an issue during your stay, you will probably not get a timely response. Evolve, a national management company, uses an automated message to respond to inquiries, which is a very long list of FAQs, as if to say to the guest, "Hey stupid, we are assuming you are asking something we already answered in the listing; don't bother us again until you read this incredibly long message full of information that is not related to your question."

We answer all inquiries with actual human answers and use automation for check-in instructions, driving directions, and post-checkout follow-ups. After someone books one of our properties, they get a message with the address, information on when they will receive their access code, and a couple reminders to have an accurate guest count and disclose any pets. We let them know in the automated message that it is an automated message to make sure they get the information they need, but a real human is monitoring the thread if they have any questions.

Financial Reporting and Listing Analytics: This is another important function of a PMS. You want to be able to quickly pull what percentage of your bookings are coming through each channel, what your ADR is, what the total nights and length of stay per channel are, etc. Financial reporting is not the strong suit of some PMS, and some lack the metrics and functionality you might expect it to have. However you choose to do bookkeeping and

track income and expenses, you want your PMS to be able to generate reports quickly and accurately, so you are more likely to check your listing health frequently and pick up on trends early on while you can still pivot. The harder it is to analyze, the less likely you are to do it; that's just part of being a lazy human.

Additional User Accounts: If you are going to be giving access to cleaners or handymen, make sure your PMS can provide additional logins with limited accessibility and that they don't charge for this or a small number of free accounts. We provide owner logins to those we manage so that they can see their listing health and monitor bookings, but we obviously limit their access to only their properties. We grant access to our cleaners specific to the units they are in charge of.

If you do not have a PMS your cleaning can log in and monitor, you will have to manually notify them of each booking.

Payment Processing and Website Builder: If you plan to have a direct booking site or handle any payment directly, you need to make sure your PMS connects to a good payment processor, and you should look into which processors they connect to and what their fees are. Our payment processor is Stripe, which is a fine vendor, but their fees are not cheap, and our PMS tacks on an additional 1% to connect with them. This is a fee that was added a couple years into our relationship that we are not happy about but are stuck with for the time being. Make sure there are options for automated payments if you are going to be taking payments.

Your PMS should also have a free website builder add-on where you can quickly and easily list your STR. Some PMS charge for this feature, some offer the means of building a full website, while others just offer a booking engine you can use on your website that will sync with the management software. Just be aware that the longer you use your PMS and the more features you build your business around, the harder it will be to switch.

THE METRICS THAT MATTER AND THE PLATFORMS THAT PERFORM

Figuring out new management software is a pain, but nothing is as painful as switching softwares, so take pains in doing your research before selecting a PMS.

Our PMS does not have good checklists or notes for cleaning, maintenance, tasks, and work orders. There is no inventory tracking at all. When we demoed multiple PMS years ago, we found Hostaway to be the most comprehensive, but it is possible there are more robust PMSs out there now. Breezeway has some good cleaning checklists, and there are some other cleaning apps that have some version of this side of the day-to-day operations, but surprisingly, no software is well-rounded in this area. It's kind of surprising that the industry is slow to have these features that are so critical to keeping your STR running smoothly. We have built our own in-house app for tracking inventory, repair requests, and maintenance checklists.

Before selecting your PMS, read reviews on how they handle customer support tickets. Many of these companies do not have phone numbers that you can call, but some of them are quite quick at answering emails and support tickets. Your software will have issues and glitches in its connectivity with OTAs, so you need a company that will be responsive. Oftentimes, when there is an issue connecting to an OTA, it is hard to determine if the PMS or the OTA is at fault, and often they both blame the other party.

You should have an overall plan of how you are going to run the day-to-day operations of your business before making a selection of software, so that you know if it offers all the connectivity you are looking for. Whether you want to integrate keyless entry, upsells, MailChimp automation, or digital rental agreements, you need to map out your plan, or you will be piecing it all together with great frustration.

If you are planning on scaling your portfolio of properties, you should also ask up front how they adjust their price with scale. Some software gives little to no discounts for having a lot of listings; some give significant breaks. If it won't work in the long term due to their price structure, do not do it in the short term.

CHAPTER 4

CUSTOMER SERVICE

Outside of selecting and setting up a property, the customer service component is the most critical piece to a successful short-term rental because the interaction between the guest and host is a major part of the guest experience. There are three parties involved in the transaction: the host, the guest, and the property. Maintain your property, take care of your guests, and you will normally have a pleasant transaction, except for the rare occasion when you receive an irrational guest.

Airbnb asks guests to give their stay an overall review out of five stars and then asks for six specific ratings for greater detail: cleanliness, accuracy, communication, location, check-in, and value. The two categories directly related to customer service are communication and check-in. If you do not excel at customer service, Airbnb is essentially prompting the guest to give you a poor rating and discourage other guests from booking your property. There is no reason to score low on either of these metrics; these are "gimmees," where you should score at least a 4.9. The other categories, especially cleanliness and value, are so much harder to maintain high scores, so you don't want to miss these easy ones.

The check-in process needs to be clear, simple, and automated. At a minimum, you should have your own system for sending specific check-in instructions before their stay. If guests have to ask for that information, that does not reflect well on

your check-in score. As long as you don't have some 1990's way of checking in, like driving somewhere to pick up the keys or meeting them on site with the keys, you should score highly here. Have a lockbox or a smart lock, send them the code, and that's all guests typically need. The only exception to this is specific driving instructions if your rental is difficult to find or if the home access is not intuitive. Several of our rentals have this, which is difficult to find, so we send detailed driving instructions two days prior to check-in. If the lockbox is not visible, or if the main entrance is a side door, spell this out in your instructions. If the guests have a hard time finding the place and attempt to check in exhausted in the middle of the night, things will go sideways in a hurry.

Our system for excelling at communication is based on the following five key principles, conveniently arranged to spell CHAOS. Chaos can't be completely eliminated, but it can be mitigated to a manageable level with the following system:

- Casual but Professional
- Holistic Understanding
- Accessible and Immediately Responsive
- Objective Perspective
- Self-service and Proactive Action

Casual but Professional

This refers to the style of communication. The host needs to utilize an informal but professional form across all communication, especially in messaging. When writing your rental agreement contract, it's okay to be formal, but on the phone and via Messenger on Airbnb, your communication should read more like a text message than a formal email. This is safe across many generations. The baby boomer generation may not mind a little more formal responses, but even that is hit or miss. Guests want to feel like they are talking to a small town host, not a desk clerk at a chain hotel.

Being overly formal makes the transaction feel transactional and less relational, which is not what you want to achieve. Is the guest more likely to leave a scathing review for an individual or for a business with whom they had a one-time transaction? They will be tougher on the business because, after all, it's just business. If they had a great experience, they would also go out of their way to write a "rave review" because they were helping out an individual who they appreciated. Being informal and personable allows you to come across as a local host. Look at an example and a few ways this can play out.

Guest: Hi Matt, I was wondering if the pool was going to be open during these dates.

Bad Response 1: As our listing states, the pool does not open until April 15th.

Bad Response 2: Jamie,

The pool will not be open. Sorry for any inconvenience this may cause your group.

Sincerely, North Georgia Vacation Rentals

Good Response 1: Hey Jamie,

Thanks for your interest in our property! Unfortunately, the pool doesn't open until April 15th. Let me know if you have any other questions or if I can help in any way.

Matt

Good Response 2: Hi Jamie,

Thanks for reaching out. Unfortunately, the pool is not heated and doesn't open until April 15th. I hope your dates are flexible if that is a deal-breaker for you! Matt

It is okay to show some personality. Since we are a company and our company logo is what the traveler is looking at on Airbnb or Vrbo, we have to work extra hard to show that we are also real humans and connect with people on a human level. If you are an individual host, this will be easier for you, but you should still focus on that connection. When people say they are staying at your rental to celebrate their 10th anniversary, tell them congratulations. When they say they will no longer be bringing their dog because they had to put it down, show some sympathy. It's not enough to just acknowledge their message; you need to respond with something that shows you internalized and processed what they actually said.

The other side of this coin is showing professionalism. I believe that, as a management company, we have a slight advantage in this regard compared to individual hosts. Because we have a company logo in our icon box on Airbnb and have many highly rated properties that we manage, we give an impression of professionalism. If you are an individual host, you will need to appear professional in every way possible, whether by emphasizing any experiences in your bio on Airbnb or just working hard to have a clearly written and professional listing, showing that you have experience hosting.

Holistic Understanding

Holistic understanding is the idea that to excel in guest communication, you have to have well-rounded experience, from the industry, to your local geography, to the property itself. This takes time, and there is no substitute for that. You can self-educate, and that will certainly help, but at the end of the day, you need the experience, and you need to understand how everything fits together. It would be unrealistic to think you would be a great host with minimal experience; that's just not how life works. You figure out how to be a good parent over time; you figure out what your spouse needs and how to serve them best over time. You can read books on parenting and marriage, and that will help, but as it turns out, individuals are different and quite complicated.

So it is with each industry. Just because you worked customer service at the counter at McDonald's in college doesn't mean you will be a five-star customer service master in the short-term rental space. Other customer service experience can certainly help, but it doesn't all translate, and you need to be careful if you try to apply a different knowledge base.

Here are some of the factors that go into the holistic understanding that is needed to provide the right answers to guests. Requests from guests lead to decisions that are tricky to balance.

Local Ordinance: Guest counts, parking rules, quiet hours, events on site, and what you can and cannot allow the guest to do on your property.

Local Recommendations: They will expect you to have a recommendation of places to eat and things to do in the area. If you don't live locally, you will need to figure this out.

Scheduling: What can your cleaners handle as far as early check-in and late check-out? Many cleaners will try to please you by accommodating everything you ask for, but will not actually be able to do a quality job if you shrink their time on site. You have to know the logistics of operations in order to make the right call.

Property-specific questions: If a breaker trips, you need to know where the breaker panel is and be able to walk the guest through resetting it. If a guest with no knowledge about how things work breaks a toilet supply line in the middle of the night and floods a basement, you need to be able to walk them through where the main shutoff is and how to turn it off (been there, done that).

You need to know where the cleaners keep extra towels on site and where the emergency supply of batteries is. The worst question to get from a guest is something simple that you should know but don't know the answer to. This does not make you look like a proactive host who has anticipated the guests' needs and cares about the user experience.

Knowing your guests: Over time, the same type of guests will book your property. Each property attracts certain types of guests. If you have a small cabin in the woods, you may have couples retreats and small families. Each type of guest will have certain goals for their trip and will be upset should they not be able to accomplish them. If a couple books the trip for use of the hot tub and the hot tub isn't working properly, you need to know how much it is upsetting them and how much to compensate them so that they don't trash you in the review. You need to be able to read into their questions and responses and get a feel for if they are confused, angry, or generally understanding and just want to give you a heads up on some things to improve for the next guests.

In regards to issues that pop up during your stay, you have to also read if the guest is just being stupid and can't figure out a basic thermostat, fireplace, or something of that nature, or if there actually is a problem. Just because the guest isn't smart enough to light the gas fireplace, even though you wrote it out clearly and specifically instructions, that doesn't mean that they are going to assume responsibility for that and won't leave you with a bad review. You have to read into the situation and know if you need to go over there and light it or compensate them for a problem they reported after they checked out and didn't give you a chance to address it. Some people can't admit when they are dumb, and some want to blame the world.

What moves the needle financially? To be a good host, you have to have a pulse on where you actually make money and whether to accept certain types of requests. Some of this gets into pricing, which will be covered later, but you have to know your numbers in order to make the right daily decisions. If a guest wants to bring extra pets, is there a risk, and at what price point is it worth it? If a guest asks for a discount during the slow season, is it worth approving? Is there a price so low that it's not worth the wear and tear on your home and having to turn the heat up in the winter? Will a low-priced guest be more likely to give you a bad review, even at a dirt-cheap price? These are the types of questions that go into the financial component specific to your market and property that are important to know to provide the right answers to guest inquiries.

Accessible and Immediately Responds

Host accessibility is an image that needs to be established from the first message and held through the end of the reservation. If a potential guest asks a question about your property, what is a reasonable time frame for a response? That is not possible to know for sure, but from experience, you have very little time to respond.

First of all, an instant response tells a guest that someone is on duty and ready to answer all questions. Even if a guest doesn't consciously connect the dots, subconsciously they are getting a good feeling about you as a host because their subconscious is assuming that you will provide the same quick response should they book your property and have an issue during their stay. If you take six hours to answer a question now, what will happen if they have an issue during their stay? Will you answer in ten minutes, or will it take six hours again when the heat goes out and they are all freezing to death? In an age where the average response time is slow to never, a quick response sets you apart. We often get guest comments like "Thanks for getting back to me so quickly," followed by a booking.

Second, a quick response may keep them from searching. Maybe they love your property and have one critical question that they need clarification on that is a deal breaker for their group. You take a couple hours to answer, and by then, they have moved on and found three other possibilities. People tend to search for properties and send out inquiries in clusters. They are looking at more properties than just yours, and sometimes they are looking to make a decision right then and there with whatever host will answer their question.

Additionally, hosting platforms track your response rate and the amount of time it takes to respond to an initial inquiry. Consistently responding within minutes during the day means that those inquiries that come in after you are asleep and don't answer until you wake up don't kill your response rate. You can still have a reassuring response rate on Airbnb that tells guests that you are a great host. I am not bragging, because this is not hard to achieve, but this is what our response rating on our listings reads on Airbnb.

Response rate: 100%

Response time: Within an hour

If you work a full-time job, you may not be able to have that response time, but you should be able to achieve that response rate.

As a property manager, I also have this same commitment to the owners I manage for. It doesn't take any more work to respond to a text message or email right away; it's not like I'm going to blow off a question or concern that an owner has regarding their property. An immediate response shows the other party that they are important to you and that you take your job seriously.

And finally, a note on accessibility. You are on call all of the time. It's possibly the toughest part of the job to not be able to throw your phone in the fridge and just spend time with your family away from the distraction of work. I've been working for seven years straight, on call 24-7. If that's not what you are prepared to do, hire a property manager. If the guest has an emergency situation and you don't pick up the phone, be prepared for a 2-star review.

Objective Perspective

As a human who answers a whole lot of travelers questions on a week to week basis, it is very easy to become accustomed to the legitimate concerns of the humans on the other end of the screen. To provide fair and consistent customer service, one has to get outside their own head, take off their manager's hat, and put on their traveler's hat. That early check-in request really does make a difference to their planning. That pack-and-play they are requesting does have an impact on how much room they have left in their SUV for the road trip. It is easy to stop being a considerate human when you get bombarded with questions every day and to slip into the mindset of doing the minimum amount of work necessary to get through the day.

But maintaining an objective perspective does not mean that the traveler is the only consideration. For you property managers out there, you have to look at every transaction through the eyes of your property owners as well. Owning properties myself and running my own rentals for years before managing for anyone else, I know this perspective well and naturally lean this way. I am not a frequent traveler, so it is more difficult for me to take the traveler's perspective. The property owner is primarily concerned with property preservation, cash flow, and reputation (reviews) that will generate future cash flow. Some property owners have slightly different objectives for their rentals, and if you manage for others, you really need to learn what is important to them in order to serve them best. Some really want to be fully hands-off (that's what they are paying us for, by the way!), while others want to be involved in a whole lot more (you are spending their money, by the way!). Some are a little obsessive about reviews and would rather refund a guest in every gray area and maintain that near-perfect rating. Some owners seemingly never check their property reviews and aren't really worried about it. Whatever the slant of the property owner, they are operating from a reasonable perspective that must be taken into account.

The other consideration, already mentioned in holistic understanding, is the viewpoint of the cleaners, handymen, lawn care companies, and others that service your property. Building and maintaining relationships with these honest and hardworking people means treating them right and not pushing them around and taking advantage of them. When you ask your lawn care company not to show up when a particular guest is on site, they have to change their entire route. When you ask the cleaner for a late check-out, that may throw off their entire day's schedule, and they might have to find someone else to pick up their kid from school. Everyone involved in the business has practical concerns and reasons for why and how they approach their business, and you must listen to these concerns, even if they are not clearly communicated, and give them permission to tell you no. For our cleaning companies, I tell them we will forward early check-in and late check-out requests and just ask them to make it work when they can, but not to do flips and mess up their entire day to accommodate. Guests know the check-in and check-out windows when they book the property, and we are not obligated to make exceptions.

At the end of the day, a good manager is the one who will take the loss when it is a choice between them and another party. A good manager has a servant's mindset and will put others, guests, employees, owners, and independent contractors above their own needs.

Self-service and Proactive Action

The burden of customer service is a combination of the number of questions received, the types of questions received, and the timing of questions received. While you can't do anything to keep travelers from asking questions at all hours of the night, you can build out your listing and information in a way that greatly reduces the total number of questions and the types of questions you receive.

Start off on the right foot with a well-written listing, with answers to the frequently asked questions spelled out in clear detail. We will go over listing descriptions in more depth later on, but this is why it is critical not to stuff your listing with fluff, because the critical details will get lost in the fluff. You don't want people to make assumptions and then ask questions after booking, or worse yet, after they have checked in. People may not even think to ask the right questions if you don't put the information out there.

For example, if you have a fire pit but do not provide firewood for campfires, disclose that clearly in the listing. People may not think to ask until they are on site, and then they are upset and you have some explaining to do. You are not trying to trick any travelers into booking with you; you are not trying to lock up their business and then make them stuck with you and unable to cancel. The goal is to get travelers who understand what the property is, what you do and don't provide, and voluntarily pay for that perceived value. If they find out after booking that the value is not what they anticipated, they are looking for reasons to complain and give you a bad review.

As a culture, we humans are so used to poor customer service that we assume it will be the case more often than not. If your listing is missing too much information and requires the traveler to ask questions, the traveler may subconsciously assume that when they arrive at your rental they won't find things well organized and laid out, and they will either have to figure things out on their own or will have to depend on you to answer questions. People don't want to depend on customer service. They are far more likely to book if they see a well-presented listing because it implies that the host has thought everything through and that everything at the rental will be equally thought out and supplied. When you are researching a product to purchase on Amazon, all things being equal, you choose the one that has more product details and specifications disclosed. The listing with a few generic bullet points makes you assume it is a cheap product, so just move on.

It is especially important to specify any fees and include anything that guests may not like in the listing. If you have an extra guest fee, disclose it in the listing, so that way if the traveler decides to bring two more guests, they aren't surprised when the price goes up by $40, or if they are, you can politely point them to the listing where you specifically disclose that fee. People will often still book without reading, so if you don't want to put yourself in a pinch, you need the not-so-fine print where you explicitly and directly state that important information.

Once your listing is live, use the frequently asked questions to help you adjust your copy and display information more clearly. Also, make sure that your digital and physical information binder stays up-to-date, is always updated, and is improved. We probably update our information binders at least 5–10 times per year.

Make sure nothing important ends up as fine print, intentionally or unintentionally. This isn't a 30-year mortgage contract where they can get away with fine print; this is a two-night stay where they will be publicly reviewing you based on your transparency. Outside of the listing description, to excel at communication, you must be proactive, be warm and friendly, and build that temporary relationship to the max. The more rapport you build, the more likely they are to show grace if there is an issue, and the more likely they are to give you a glowing review if everything goes well. The way you build rapport is to be proactive at all points of the transaction. If they book without any inquiries or questions, send them a personal note, welcoming them and answering any questions they may have. Often, guests will let you know why they are staying, such as "coming into town for my son's wedding." When they do that, which means they are looking for a personal connection with their host, and they expect a reciprocal mindset. If they booked a hotel, they wouldn't call and tell the receptionist this; they are choosing the short-term rental experience in part because of the personalization, so be as proactive in communication as they are.

It is also good to check in (manually or with careful automation) a couple days prior to their arrival, with a reminder about check-in, and again offer assistance if they need anything. After their stay, make sure to check back in, preferably before they are able to leave a review, asking for any feedback about the property. We will cover more detail about this step in the review management section, but being proactive in customer service requires showing the guest you actually want to know if there was anything that was not perfect with their stay. If they give you feedback and you make a quick repair or schedule the repair, let them know that. They will be less likely to mention it in a review if they know you were proactive about it, and it shouldn't be a problem for the next guest. You can gather this feedback through the OTA they booked on, through text, paper surveys on site, digital surveys sent at check-out, or phone calls. The more personal and the more immediate, the more effective.

Another component of being proactive is making sure that you are crystal clear in your communication. Guests often are very vague and discombobulated in their messaging, and it is very difficult to ascertain what they are even asking or saying, and it takes a lot of experience and sometimes a bit of luck to make enough sense of it to know how to answer. Make sure you are not doing the same to them and stating things that can be interpreted in different ways, or leave them with ambiguity on what the expectation is. For example, if they are wondering if they can check in early and you can accommodate so long as you don't get a last-minute booking, don't just say, "As long as nobody else books, that is fine." Instead, give the complete picture, everything that they need to know in order to make travel arrangements.

Early check-in is available so long as someone else doesn't book the night before your arrival, in which case we likely will not be able to get you in early. If you check back with us after 11:00 a.m. the day before your stay, we can confirm that nobody has booked and early check-in is available. We do have an early check-in fee of $25 per hour.

And finally, the last word on being proactive in communication is getting the last word in. Giving the last response shows that you have noted their message, either good or bad. There are a few rare exceptions to this rule, but as a principle, you want to acknowledge receipt of everything they say. If it is negative feedback, tell them thanks for the information so you can make it right. If it is positive or neutral, acknowledge it in a friendly way. Many times, I will just shoot over the thumbs-up emoji. You want to have the last message sent, so when they pull up the message thread again to send you a message, they see you were the last to message, and they are reminded of your excellent customer service.

CHAPTER 5

CLEANING AND MAINTENANCE

The cleaning and maintenance of your property is a significant portion of the daily grind that can become overwhelming to hosts, or worse, become neglected as the priority that they should be. Both cleaning and maintenance are critical to the bottom line as well as the guest experience. Cleaning and maintenance are not the same, but they are under a similar umbrella, so we will address them in the same chapter.

It is not fair to expect your cleaning person to also handle maintenance, unless you have discussed this with them and are compensating them for the extra work. If you can find someone who is capable and willing to do both, this can be a valid strategy. I call this a "cleaning plus" strategy, but you should expect to look harder and pay more for someone who is qualified and willing to take that on. You may also be able to find a husband and wife team that together will act as a "cleaning plus" team and therefore reduce the communication and complexity of using two separate parties.

CLEANING AND MAINTENANCE

In the ideal world, it is a better strategy to have two separate positions: a cleaning position and a maintenance and inspection position. If only one person is in the rental on a day to day basis, they will become blind to what needs to be done and do an excellent job on some things but miss other things. Having someone with industry experience and a fresh set of eyes walking through on a routine basis is a game changer. As the old saying goes, "Old eyes and fresh eyes are the best eyes."

For the majority of our homes, we contract out the cleaning to a top-notch cleaning company and then have our employees go behind them as much as possible and conduct inspections. Our inspectors are looking for three main things:

- Quality of the cleaning, catching any little mistakes the cleaners might make, and fixing them on the spot.
- Checking for overall presentation. The property may be clean, but there may be an odd thing or two that isn't quite right. For example, a double window with one blind open and one blind closed is not a cleaning error per se, but it is not ideal from a presentation standpoint.

- Looking at maintenance and repair items. Our inspectors fix any small items on the spot, and take notes for tool and material lists while on site for larger projects.

Most DIY managers who are local will be their own inspectors, possibly their own cleaner, and most can't afford to pay a separate person to come in and do inspections. There are some STR inspection companies out there that are trying to capitalize on the out of town DIY managers, but they focus more on the physical maintenance side of the inspection and are not going to inspect for presentation and cleaning standards. You can get a handyman to check out your home and check for rotted deck boards, clogged downspouts, and doors that don't close properly, but getting someone to inspect things from a guest perspective takes someone with some industry perspective.

If you are going to go for a cleaning plus strategy, you need to take your time and find someone who is thorough and detail-oriented and not in a hurry. Find someone who does laundry on site, who likes to go slow, takes pride in their work, and is not rushed. You need to know who is actually going to be cleaning the rental. Many cleaning companies use subcontractors, and the owner or head cleaner may clean the rental the first few times to establish a checklist and then turn it over to a lower-paid contractor or employee with a lot less experience. This is reasonable from their perspective; they have to make money and stay in business. But if you are out of state, you cannot have someone making $14 an hour working a side job in college and being responsible for making sure your rental is guest - ready. Many head cleaners will come back through properties to catch errors by lower-paid employees, but that is not likely to happen on a busy day full of same-day turnovers, and hoping to catch errors is not the same as doing things with excellence all the time. At the end of the day, results are all that matters, and if whoever you hire is able to consistently crank out a solid job, you should not be overly concerned with their business model, but it is always a good idea to know what is actually going on at your property.

What is and is not included needs to be discussed upon interviewing a cleaner and before you agree on a price. Here are a few things outside of standard cleaning that we think are reasonable to expect from a cleaner:

- Heat/AC on and set to a reasonable temperature

CLEANING AND MAINTENANCE

- Notification of damage or anything not working properly
- Hot tubs set at the right temperature and in the right mode
- Notification if supply is low
- Windows and doors are locked
- Outdoor furniture is wiped down
- Trash immediately around the house was picked up

Here are some examples of some gray areas that will need to be discussed and made clear with a cleaner up front:

- Changing light bulbs.
- Blowing off porches of dust and pollen, knocking down cobwebs in doorways and windows.
- Cleaning and removing trash in the yard on a large property, especially with a playground and outdoor games.
- Changing batteries in remotes and smoke detectors.
- Cleaning up after excessively dirty guests without charging extra.
- Being compensated for showing up and waiting for guests to check out, or having to

come back because a guest has not checked out on time.

Here are some examples that you should not expect them to do at all without compensation:

- Resupply, ordering or picking up supplies
- Changing HVAC filters
- Mailing left-behind items
- Hauling off trash
- Troubleshooting the internet
- Meeting technicians or contractors

Be clear and honest with whoever you are interviewing for cleaning; you are shooting for a stress-free, long-term, healthy relationship. If you do not have experience in the STR space, ask, "What am I not thinking to ask you?"

You will need to go over check-in and check-out times and negotiate availability up front. You need to know if they have any restrictions on their calendar and make sure they can handle same-day turnovers and have seven-day-a-week availability.

Depending on your market, you may not be able to find someone who is affordable, thorough, and available; you may have to pick two of the three. It is generally preferable to pay a little more for quality, especially if you are managing from a

CLEANING AND MAINTENANCE

distance and do not have someone regularly going by after cleanings to perform inspections.

Ask for pricing up front and determine if a fixed fee or hourly rate is best for both of you. Some cleaners that are used to working for high-end residential clients are very, very expensive and don't have a realistic expectation of what you can collect in a cleaning fee. We have received quotes for over twice what we had our market-rate cleaning fee set at.

Ask the potential cleaner what they charge for other rentals they clean, and look around at other local STRs and see what the average cleaning fee is for similar properties. If you are going for a cleaning plus strategy, hourly may be simpler, so you can just have them do extra projects as needed without complicating things. Overall, a fixed fee is the industry norm and works better. If it is at all possible, hire cleaners with STR experience, not just residential or commercial experience, and definitely not one without any experience.

Sometimes guests do leave rentals excessively dirty, and cleaners expect to be compensated for extra work, but beware of cleaners who consistently ask for more than the agreed-upon cleaning fee. It is difficult for a host to bill the guest an additional cleaning fee and not get a bad review from them. Every guest thinks the cleaning fee they paid was already too expensive and thinks they left the place in good condition. I have had guests leave trash all over the place, leave the kitchen blown up with nasty dishes, and then tell us they hope we appreciated the great condition they left the property in. You're not going to get away with tacking on $50 to every guest that doesn't pick up after themselves; both you and your cleaners need to know it's just part of the business and to just deal with it. It is the luck of the draw on guests; some are very clean and leave the house almost as clean as when they arrived; some touch every surface in the house with greasy hands and pull everything out of drawers and rearrange all the decor in the house.

How often cleaners need to be paid is important as well. Someone who needs to be paid after every turn is probably not in a healthy financial state, and that may cause problems. It will also increase your admin and bookkeeping significantly if they need to be paid frequently. One of our two cleaning vendors does insist we pay weekly so she can make payroll, but she sends professional invoices, keeps our card on file, and takes care of it for us.

Ideally, cleaners will send a professional invoice once a month and will not be pressing you with a Venmo request twice a week.

Communication with your cleaners is absolutely critical. If a potential cleaner is not communicating well before hiring them, do not even consider them. The worst case scenario is guests wanting to check in early, and you can't even get confirmation from the cleaner on whether they have even showed up and cleaned yet. Quick and clear communication is a must in this industry; if someone doesn't understand that, they won't make it as a cleaner, and you do not want to do business with them.

Cleaners should have access to your calendar, and you should not have to text them the schedule every day. We grant our cleaners access to our PMS and message them about any schedule changes, whether that be contractors who may be at the property when they are, a new booking, or cancellations that are less than seven days out. Anything more than seven days out, we expect them to notice calendar changes and be able to do their own planning and scheduling.

It is also best practice for cleaners to supply their own cleaning supplies. Typically, they want to do so anyway because they want to use products and tools they know work since they are responsible for the end result. Consumables that the guests use, like trash bags, hand soap, and dish soap, are not cleaning supplies that your cleaner should have to provide.

The last critical piece of cleaning is linens. Whatever your strategy is around linens, you need to have spare linens available for guests. Some cleaners prefer to wash on site, and some prefer to do it offsite. Some prefer to do sheets and towels offsite, but comforters and bath mats are on site. Whatever the strategy is, have backups on site so that there are no hang-ups that can cause the home not to be ready by the agreed-upon check-in time. If someone stains a comforter, you don't need someone to make an emergency run to the store to get one before check-in; you want to just throw on the backup and have some time to attempt to get the stain out of the nicer comforter before trying to bill the guest and buy a new one. This business has enough time constraints; you don't need to add more by trying to save a few bucks (that you will have to spend anyway) on additional towels and sheets.

CLEANING AND MAINTENANCE

If you are going to be cleaning the rental yourself, here is the cleaning tool kit that we give our employees.

- Hot Tub Strainer
- Hot Tub Vacuum
- Hot Tub Pump
- Laundry Bags (dirty and clean)
- Corded Vacuum
- Cordless Hand Vac
- Mop, bucket, or pads
- Broom and Dustpan
- Microfiber clothes
- Paper Towels
- Disinfectant
- All-purpose cleaner
- Glass Cleaner
- Cleaning Caddy
- Sos/Green Scour Pad
- Magic Erasers
- Toilet Seals
- Scraper
- Toilet Bowl Cleaner
- Stainless steel cleaner
- Dusting Kit with an Extended Handle
- Fabric and Rug Stain Remover
- Step Stool

CLEANING AND MAINTENANCE

Properly cleaning a STR could be a book in and of itself, but I will just go into some basics as well as some common errors and issues. Even if you are not going to be the one cleaning your rental, it will make you a better manager and give you respect for your cleaners if you do it yourself once or twice. It is not an easy job; there are a million details that can be easily missed, and just one missed hair on a sink can sink you if it happens to a certain type of guest. I clean properties several times a year, sometimes scheduled, sometimes in an emergency, and it helps me stay engaged in that side of the business and helps me be grateful to our cleaners.

Your cleaner needs to have a can-do attitude and be a go-getter. If you have to tell them every little thing, find someone else. Some people get it, some don't, and more time won't fix people who don't get it after a couple of weeks. Our best cleaner is one that has also managed short-term rentals, and I don't think that is a coincidence.

Industry experience is a huge help; some people travel often and use short-term rentals and can see what may matter to guests. Others just can't see things, and there is literally nothing you can do to fix that.

The order in which you clean matters. The first things you want to focus on are the time-sensitive things, the ones that you can only do so quickly and can get stuck waiting on at the end. For us, that includes hot tubs, the dishwasher, and laundry if we do laundry on site. So we teach our cleaners to go straight to the hot tub and start draining it if necessary, then flip laundry and make sure the dishwasher has been run.

After that, the order doesn't matter all that much, unless you are violating a common sense thing like dusting after you swept and mopped. Normally I will dust as I go around and turn on all the lights and get an overall scope of how messy the guests left the place and how much work I have cut out with me. You would be surprised at how many cleaners clean in the dark and then are surprised when they miss things. Once I was helping out a cleaning vendor that was struggling, and I turned on the living room lights when I saw she was sweeping and mopping in the dark. Five minutes later, I came back into the room, and she had turned the lights back off and was still mopping. You can't get what you can't see, so just turn on every light available if you want to do a good job.

CLEANING AND MAINTENANCE

After dusting, I typically work in the kitchen and bathrooms, as they are the biggest consumers. I usually make all the beds toward the end and sweep and mop my way out.

There are a few tips for each space that are not commonly taught.

Bedrooms

- Make sure you move the nightstand and check for trash or strange items left in the drawers.
- Dust the fixtures, especially a ceiling fan over a bed, before taking off the linens to wash them.
- Make sure you check under the bed every time.
- Turn on the lamps, because you will find them unplugged 40% of the time. Bathroom:
- Spray the tub or shower early, and let it sit a minute while you work on something else.
- Use a vacuum to suck up hairs instead of chasing them around with your cleaning rag or sponge.
- Focus on the toilet and the entirety of the toilet. Don't forget to wipe down the toilet base, and don't leave nasty water in the toilet scrub brush.

- You can do the vanity mirrors as you go or do them as a separate item when you do the windows. Dawn dish soap diluted with water works just as well as Windex.

Kitchen

- Check every cabinet and every drawer every time. We get complaints from improperly washed dishes from previous guests, so everything has to be spot checked, and some items need to be pulled back out and rewashed.
- Don't be OCD with organization, but if your cabinets look like four year old put away dishes, straighten things up and put matching sets together. Make sure you are vacuuming and wiping out the inside of the drawers and cabinets, and wiping down the face of the cabinets as well.
- Generally, you want to scrub the sink last and take the trash out at the end. If you have a habit of forgetting to take the trash out, hang the bag from the doorknob on the front door so you can keep using it until the end, but don't miss it on your way out.

These things are just the tip of the iceberg. Should you give your cleaners a comprehensive checklist?

CLEANING AND MAINTENANCE

Probably not. If they are good, they will have some version of their own. We give our employee cleaners a very basic reminder checklist. I have seen checklists over a hundred items long. This will not actually be used; the cleaner will just check a bunch of boxes when they are done without reading it.

We have an app we built through Jotform for our cleaners, so they can upload photos, report damage, and let us know when the home is complete. The checklist in the app just has a few reminders for each area of the house, not a comprehensive list.

For example, the Kitchen column has "All dishes checked" and "Kitchen supplies available, sponges, trash bags, etc. We don't put a clean toaster, a clean fridge, and a clean microwave on an exhaustive list.

At the end of the checklist, we make them check the following as a general reminder:

The furniture is in the correct location.

Everything is presentable.

I have walked through the unit and looked everything over, and I didn't just follow the checklist like a robot. This house is ready.

We do not require or want photos or videos after a cleaning showing that the cleaning is complete. I know that is fairly common now, but you can't tell if someone nailed the details with photos and videos, and I don't have time to watch a video walkthrough every time a home is clean. You can't see a hair that was missed on a toilet in a video; there is no point in wasting anyone's time doing that madness. I doubt that video is enough to win an argument with Airbnb and avoid a refund if the guest complains about cleaning.

<u>Inspections and maintenance:</u>

Inspections and maintenance are the next component of a well-cared for property that must be intentionally planned for and executed. If you are using a cleaning plus strategy, make sure that this does not fall by the wayside and that you set expectations for what parts of the home should be regularly inspected and accomplished outside of the day to day cleaning items. The maintenance component cannot be as casual as telling your cleaners, "If you see something that is broken, let me know," or "If you notice the air filter is dirty, please change it out for me."

Maintenance and repairs seem to come in waves. This is yet another reason why it is important to stack cash when things go well. You can go four or five months with barely any maintenance or repair expenses, and then the next month you schedule a pressure washing and deck staining because it's slow season, and your fridge quits and the garage roof leaks in the same month. Be grateful for the quiet spells, but be prepared to tolerate the furries as well.

In our small company, our managers split time with our handyman to do the weekly walkthroughs. The two main skills that are needed for this position are:

- STR experience: knowing what guests complain about, so you know what to monitor and prioritize.
- Repair and maintenance experience: knowing when something is not right and being able to fix small things on the spot.

When inspecting properties, we are looking for:

- Presentation: Anything that is not presentable for a guest. Things may be clean but left out and looking cluttered. The junk drawer may need to be cleaned out. The board games may have loose pieces that need to be put away. A guest will not complain about one or two small things like this that are not perfect, but if everywhere they look, it seems like there is a lack of attention to detail, it will be reflected in the review. At the same time, you can't be obsessive about every detail that doesn't move the needle. If a picture is significantly crooked, yes, straighten it. But you don't need to organize the games every time, arrange the silverware a certain way, or chop the top of the pillow on every bed and couch. If you are focusing on that, you aren't focusing on what does matter.

- Cleanliness: We try to do our walkthrough inspections after cleaning has been done, unless there is a large repair or maintenance project to be done. We have a cleaning inspection form on our app so that the cleaners can see how they did and read any notes the inspector had for things they missed. You better find an inspector who is willing to clean behind the cleaner and do what needs to be done, which includes getting down on their hands and knees to check under beds and tables. Kids and babies are going to get low, so your inspector better be willing to get low to see if the cleaners got low.

Whoever is giving feedback to the cleaner needs to have a friendly disposition and make sure it is done in a good way. The written word can be interpreted in many different ways, so that text or email can be taken as more aggressive and aggravated than you intended. Don't burden them with the small stuff. Unless it is a consistent or fairly major error, just correct it and move on.

- Routine maintenance: Properly maintaining the property is important in regards to extending the lifespan of the property and maximizing value, and it is also forward-facing to the guests. Every property is different and should have a customized inspection list. Don't assume that your maintenance person is going to remember to open the crawl space vents in the spring; you must have a detailed list for your property.
- Repairs and Projects: Major repairs require a significant amount of administration. Typically, any significant work requires

multiple bids, scheduling, coordinating with the owner, and blocking the calendar for an appropriate amount of time. A project on an active STR is not like a repair on your personal home where you can allow someone to repair your home with you in it. To decrease revenue loss, all this needs to be planned for with as much possible lead time, which means catching these things early so you have time to schedule them in the slow season or lowest performing weekdays. Small repairs should be done by the inspector on site, if he or she is qualified. If at all possible, don't put little petty items on a to-do list; just do it and be done with it.

Within our operations, the inspector and handyman position also encompasses doing inventory and restocking supplies. We will take an inventory of the supplies on one visit and restock them out of the supplies at our shop on our next visit to the property. I will go into detail on supplies in chapter nine.

Here is an example of some checklists that we run through for each property and the frequency of these checks. For each property, we modify the list, adding anything that is specific to the property and needs to be monitored.

Every time Checklist:

Landscaping and exteriors are presentable; porches are blown off; trash is picked up

Brief walk through of every room, looking for anything out of place and damaged

Check windows are latched and storm windows are closed

Trash is hauled to the road or hauled off

Furniture, decor, and household items in the right place

Anything property specific needs to be checked (pool or hot tub maintenance). Thermostat set correctly (Fan set to Auto, 71 degrees summer, 68 degrees winter if near check-in time)

Dehumidifier emptied (where applicable)

Check for spare propane tanks

Check the firepit for excessive ash and pick up any trash

CLEANING AND MAINTENANCE

Perform a cleaning inspection if the property is already cleaned, fix any errors, and report to management

Monthly Checklist:

Extra Supplies check

HVAC filter check

Light bulb check

Furniture check

Remotes work

Survey Sheets available

Look under vanities for damage

Check drawers

Clean up the board game area

Check the grill for rust and cleanliness

Gutter cleaning and pressure wash assessment

Check Mailbox

Septic Flush

Vanity, dresser, and end table drawers

Check under beds

Fire extinguishers were checked

CLEANING AND MAINTENANCE

Sponges, quality, and extra out

Check battery smoke and carbon monoxide detectors

3-4x Year:

Junk drawers and kitchen cabinet surpluses were cleaned out

Kitchenware checked for damaged or crappy utensils

First aid kit checked and restocked

Door Mat Quality and Quantity

Leather cleaning: inspect or do

Quality and quantity of towels (bath, pool, dish, hand, and washcloths)

Check the wired smoke and carbon monoxide detectors.

2x A Year:

Kitchen inventory and quality check

Check the quantity and quality of pillows

Flush Rootkill (April and August)

It is important to have someone who has both good attention to detail and the skills to fix what needs to be fixed but doesn't get bogged down in things that don't matter. It is a position of detail but also a position of hustle, or you will end up paying a very high bill when your inspector is there for six hours four times a month.

If you create a checklist for your inspector, it is important that they don't become robots and just go by the list, but utilize common sense, notice, and complete necessary tasks outside the list. Just as with cleaning, you can't build a perfect checklist, and if you could, it would be fourteen miles long, and any good inspector would refuse to touch it.

Region and property specific knowledge plays a key role in developing a good list as well. Most of our properties are on septic systems, which are expensive to the owner and very inconvenient to the guests if they fail or even if they need to be pumped.

These types of failures usually create a catastrophe of an expense, usually involving both a weekend service call and a refund to the guest. We flush septic treatment packs monthly because we know that guests will flush things they shouldn't and could overload the tank. Since routinely flushing these, we have only had septic issues related to

122 | **YOUR NET DETERMINES YOUR NET**

clogs due to feminine products, which is good because a standard tank pumping costs about $700 now. It is also common in our area for trees to grow back up in the septic field and invade the drain lines, so we flush Root Kill twice a year to keep the lines clear. The Root Kill product should have copper sulfate as the active ingredient, not sodium chloride. As with most products, the brand name doesn't matter. Replacing septic lines costs about $4,000 to $6,000 and requires shutting down your rental. Every property and geographic area calls for specific maintenance, so figure out what your property requires so you don't pay for mishaps that could have been avoided.

It seems that every owner or property manager tends to focus a little too much on either the customer facing side of maintenance or on the asset protection side of maintenance. The customer facing side of maintenance includes things like keeping up with pressure washing, keeping the shrubs trimmed back, keeping doors oiled, and opening and closing properly. On the asset protection side of maintenance are items like HVAC maintenance and septic maintenance, things that hurt the bottom line but that the guests won't necessarily care about unless a system fails while they are there. Some items fall into both categories, such as staining a deck to preserve the wood and keep a neat appearance for guests. It is difficult to find the right balance and spend the right amount of money in the right area. It is very helpful to buy or build a property with a low-maintenance design and to make sure you have someone with the right priorities and mindset in charge of your property's maintenance. I have seen homes with HVAC filters missing entirely when we took them over, and some with filters that hadn't been changed in over a year. I've seen rotting deck boards and a ton of clogged gutters and downspouts, but I have also seen homes with unnecessary expenses that skyrocketed the overhead of the property and crimped profit margins. You can't afford to pressure wash your home four times a year and have your trees and lawn sprayed for fungus and every other service that vendors try to sell you. You just can't let everyone have a piece of your wallet.

One of the biggest variables in maintenance that does not seem to get a lot of attention is landscaping. I actually own a landscaping company, which I turned over to one of my employees five years ago, so I am very familiar with the work and expense that goes into maintaining a property that is not designed for low maintenance. In our market, people are wanting to get out into the woods and nature, and cutting back the woods, planting a sod lawn, and having extensive ornamental garden beds do little to nothing to enhance the guest experience. It does, however, add a significant amount of direct overhead as well as increase the scheduling and coordination needed to maintain them.

When you are making material choices, use permanent materials like river rock or rubber mulch as often as possible. Stone may be more expensive, but it is usually equivalent to about three mulch installations. Don't go crazy with planting shrubs and trees that have to be pruned twice a year. Make sure your drainage, especially your downspouts and driveway drainage, is properly planned and executed, or you will have more expensive issues to deal with. If you have garden beds, make them simple with a few plants and accent boulders, not a lot of groundcover and perennials that have to be weeded by hand. You want your landscaping contractor to be able to breeze through with their backpack sprayer of Roundup, or they will charge you an arm and a leg.

CLEANING AND MAINTENANCE

Use landscaping fabric whenever possible, and don't try to be cheap and skip the edging, or your rock or mulch will continually wash out of the bed.

We do occasionally get complaints when the landscaping is serviced during a guest stay, so if possible, let your guests know the service will be stopping by, and do not let the landscaping service during any non-standard hours, such as early in the morning, on weekends, or holidays. For the most part, people understand when a service comes by from 8:00–5:00 Monday through Friday.

If you design your space wisely and stay on top of your maintenance regularly, you will be just fine. If you don't, the tail will be wagging the dog before you know it.

CHAPTER 6

THE TOUGH STUFF

In this chapter, we will tackle some of the most difficult situations that arise in the STR industry. Before we launch into it, let me say that, in my opinion, the best way to do hard stuff is to make someone else do it. Well, that's my pitch for professional management.

A lot of the difficulty is related to a lack of information. You would think that in today's age, information would be readily available and easily accessible, but when dealing with local governments and Home Owners Associations, it is not always so. There is often a good bit of difficulty in attaining a STR license. We operate in an area with limited regulation (there are pros and cons to that) and a pretty helpful planning department, but the rules and process are always changing as the industry has grown and as complaints have come in and restrictions have gone into effect.

Information is the best stress reducer, so it is important that you directly contact your local government and read all of the requirements for short-term licensing before purchase. Rules also change; it is important that you assess whether it is reasonable to expect that your property is "grandfathered in" to any changes in the rules that would disqualify it for licensing. One of the properties that we manage had a major change in ordinances two days after purchase, before we even had time to acquire a short-term rental license. STRs were being outlawed in that particular zoning, and by the time we confirmed the changes with our local government, we had until the end of the next business day to launch the listing and get a booking in order to be grandfathered in. We got it done, because getting stuff done is what we do, but it was a stressful period for us and the property owners.

Local officials and governments get so many complaints about STRs that they are often hesitant to answer anything they are not 100% sure of. You will need to press them for direct answers and ask to be transferred to their supervisor, who can give you a direct answer about rules and licensing if you can't get clear information. You will need to use all your people's skill and power as nice humans to get the right information.

Some governments don't police their short-term rentals at all, and where we operate is still a bit of the wild west. There are many in our county still without a license, allowing events on their property, guest counts that far exceed the limit, and whatever other rules they feel like violating. These types of listings can be hard to compete with, so be sure to factor STR rules and rule enforcement into your selection of an area to invest in.

Dealing with a homeowners association can be extremely difficult as well. If you are in a rural market, I would encourage you, if at all possible, to purchase or build outside of a community. Even if the community is STR-friendly, there are challenges that come with being exposed to certain community variables, such as noise, grumpy and nosy old retired people, traffic, shared water systems, and shared community amenities. The more variables that are outside of your control, the higher your exposure to uncontrollable situations, which will increase the amount of work you must put in to decrease the risk of bad reviews. We have two cabins in a community that is on a shared well system, where they always seem to be working on the well. Without any notice, we will be told, "Oh, by the way, the well is being worked on and the water is turned off, and when it comes back on, your guests will have to boil water until it can be tested to see if it is safe." It is very difficult to keep guests happy with unexpected changes, so you really need to assess the risks to communities.

Even in communities where STRs aren't restricted, many times the residents are not happy about it. This is the case in three of the other cabins we manage. Oftentimes, there is nothing in the covenants that restricts STRs, probably because they were written decades before STRs were popular, and it takes a lot of work to get the majority of the HOA on board with ratifying any changes to the covenants. So the retired, grumpy old man next door who doesn't want "those Airbnb parties" makes it his life's goal to be a thorn in your side. Oh, and by the way, he has a dog that won't stop barking and often lets it run loose on your property. So just because you are allowed to operate within an HOA doesn't mean you will be able to do so trouble-free. Distance from neighbors and privacy is a huge risk reduction and should be prioritized when seeking a property.

If the covenants are not clear on whether you can operate a STR in the community, be doubly cautious. Our local government does not weigh in on interpreting community covenants, so they will go ahead and issue the license as long as the owner signs an affidavit stating that they are allowed to operate a STR in the community. If the HOA disagrees, they can pursue a civil suit in court. There are communities that are very clearly open to STRs, have active STRs, and are even designed with amenities for STRs. There is no reason to select a property in a gray area; just choose one where the legality of operating a STR is clear and you can put your energy into creating a great product, not playing defense and worrying about fighting with neighbors or the local government to avoid being shut down.

Establishing good relations with the neighbors takes work and intentional action. Before buying or building, go and talk to the neighbors. A neighbor is anyone within shouting distance of your property. I've gotten complaints from folks 500 feet away. When the leaves fall off the trees in the winter, the sound carries like it's on open water. And that goes both ways. Your guests will complain about the neighbors shooting guns, having a party, or barking dogs just as much as the other way around.

Be honest with your neighbor about your intent with the property, but also explain to them the rules you have in place about quiet hours and your plan for removing guests should they violate the rules. If you are installing cameras or noise sensors, tell your neighbor that. Clearly mark property lines to reduce trespassing. Give the neighbors your 24-7 contact number, or the contact number of your property manager if you are hiring out the management. You want their complaint to come to you or your property manager, not straight to law enforcement or STR enforcement. If you set up your listing and your rules correctly, you should not have a significant number of complaints, but you still want to be the first contact from the neighbor. Most local governments have a set number of strikes before large fines or license suspensions, so if you can head off any complaints, that will be to your advantage.

Another difficulty that may or may not apply to you is staying up-to-date on current sales tax. If you are a small operator and do not have a direct booking website, most likely you will have little involvement in regards to remitting sales tax.

Make sure your accounts on your OTAs (Airbnb, Vrbo, etc.) have your correct tax rates and bed fees for the county in which you reside, and they should handle remitting those taxes for each booking. If you are taking bookings directly or are the payment processor for any of your OTAs, you need to put in a whole lot more work into figuring out how to remit taxes and track everything properly. States and local governments can change rates and fees at any time, and if you miss a change, you could be in a world of hurt. In my county, we are on our third tax increase on sales tax since I opened up my first STR.

Sales tax can be a bit of a problem with guests as well. We have had guests argue with us that their pet fee should not be taxable. We often get inquiries from inexperienced travelers who say, "My rate on Airbnb was this, but my out-of-door price is way higher. What is going on?" This is normally a combination of the website booking fee and taxes, which jump the traveler's price by roughly 20–25%, depending on the local government. OTA traveler fees tend to hit at about 8–12 percent, and our local tax rates hit at 16% plus $5 per night. I hate hitting guests for the extra taxes, and we choose to eat the taxes ourselves on early check-in fees because we think it would make the guest feel as if we were nickeling and diming them to charge a couple bucks extra on a $20 early check-in fee. We do charge taxes on manually collected pet fees, as that is too much to pay out of our pocket.

Now that we have established the right approach and mindset for customer service in Chapter 4, we need to narrow in on the toughest things to address on the customer service side; early check-ins and late checkouts, and cancellation requests.

I put both of these in the tough stuff category because they essentially cannot be made easy, no matter how experienced you are or how excellent your systems and policies are. Traveling humans have a lot of variables in their schedule, and that puts variability back into your schedule to try to accommodate their requested changes. Traveling humans have a lot of anxiety before and during their trip, so you are dealing with people on edge. This anxiety is also compounded if the purpose of their trip has a high degree of associated stress; for example, if you are dealing with the mother of the bride planning a wedding from 800 miles away or someone hosting a conference or event. All these human variables mean that you need to relate to them on a human level, understand their real and perceived needs, and have your policies clear and your systems firing on all cylinders so you are prepared to handle anything that gets thrown at you.

Early check-in is the most common request that we get, and it accounts for a significant percentage of our customer service work. For us, the most common reasons why guests "need" an early check-in are:

- Weddings, need to get in and get dressed for the rehearsal dinner at a fixed time
- Coming from a long drive with kids and just need to land at a destination as soon as possible so the kids can nap or crash
- Need to drop off groceries in the fridge
- Need to get in and decorate the property before the birthday person arrives
- No reason given; they just want in early, especially on one-night stays; they want extra value for what they are paying

Occasionally we get people who don't want to actually check in early but want to drop off vehicles so they can start their wine tour or drop stuff off in the fridge before they go to an event. These requests are even more frustrating for the host because you can't really charge an early check-in fee for a vehicle parked in the driveway, but you still have to do all the work of communicating with the guest and cleaners, making sure the cleaners are okay with it and don't get their vehicle blocked in. Cleaners are often not comfortable being in the house with strangers and don't want strangers coming in to put groceries in the fridge while they are vacuuming with their backs to the door.

There is a significant amount of trickiness in regards to early check-in on top of the extra work and coordination. First, you can't promise guests early check-in unless you are certain you are not going to get a last-minute booking for the night before. This year, we have seen travelers booking more last-minute than ever, making it fairly likely that someone is going to decide on a last-minute getaway. So on the one hand, you have someone who books the property 90 days out, asking for an early check-in before the wedding, but you know that while right now the calendar is vacant and you know your cleaners will have it ready, you can't approve a 1:00 check-in if there is any chance of getting a last-minute booking and a guest checking out at 10:00 that morning.

Most guests understand why we can't approve an early check-in so far in advance if you explain it to them, but there is some irritation from other guests.

It doesn't help guests plan if they don't know whether or not early check-in will be available.

This is the basic message that we send to guests.

Hi Jane,

Early check-in is available as long as someone else doesn't book the night before your arrival, in which case we likely cannot get you in early. If you check back with us after 11:00 am the day before your stay, we can confirm that nobody has

booked and an early check-in is available. As I'm sure you saw in the listing, we do have an early check-in fee of $25 per hour. Thanks,

Matt

Obviously, you should clearly post your early check-in and late check-out fees on your list, if you have any. Make sure you remind your guests about it whenever they message you about early check-in. Always assume they won't read the listing; you don't want them to be frustrated with a surprise fee and accuse you of hiding it in the fine print. About 20% of the time, we get a response like, "What? There is a fee. Never mind then".

Having an early check-in fee and posting it clearly in your listing accomplishes several things. Most importantly, it reduces the number of people who will request early check-in. Many people do not want to pay for it and won't ask about it if they see that it costs them money. It also sets the tone for the property, saying that everything is clearly stated, reasonable, and thought out, but this property is run like a business, and we expect people to pay for extended use. We think this helps us attract the type of guests that we want, namely travelers who aren't looking for the cheapest everything and then will make unreasonable demands, but those who want quality accommodations and a predictable user experience. Occasionally, we still get people who book a property and say they need to be in by noon without asking if that would be possible before booking. After we tell them, we can't guarantee that they normally cancel as long as they are within their free cancellation window. If not, the relationship is immediately rocky, and we have a troubled guest.

Charging an early check-in fee is work in and of itself, and years ago, I used to just tell people they could check in early if they wanted to. However, coordinating all the early check-ins was becoming a burden on us and the cleaners, so to compensate our owners for extra time at the property and to compensate ourselves for the additional work ourselves, we added the fee. The fee is also justifiable because the cleaners often have to modify the schedule, and the property is being used for a longer period of time, so you will have higher utilities and wear and tear.

Occasionally, guests will push the boundaries of paying for extra time and booking an extra day. We have had guests want to check in at 1:00 in the morning but want to consider that an early check-in and not an extra night. We have also had requests to stay until 4:00 or 5:00 p.m. Both of these should be rejected and charged the full night because they are making those other days unbookable. If you are in a slow season and are not likely to get that extra day booked, you can block off the date and sell it to them for around the price of half a day. Also, hosts should be wary of late arrivals. I would not turn down a booking because someone wants to arrive in the middle of the night, but make sure the property is easy to locate in the dark and they have confirmed they have received and understood the check-in instructions.

Other early check-in issues include a very high percentage of guests thinking they need to arrive early but then get stuck in traffic or run late and don't end up arriving early. You will do a lot of the work by coordinating with the cleaners and guests, and then they will show up two hours after normal check-in. Do not send payment requests or charge their credit card until they have confirmed they have arrived early. Smart locks and cameras are helpful here in determining when guests actually arrive; otherwise, you will have to trust them to self-report.

Even so, you will get pushback on fees, and I would occasionally recommend making exceptions and waiving them. We have had guests tell us the day of their arrival that they need to arrive early, and after we confirm they can do so and remind them of the fee, they call us and ask us on the phone for an exception. When you are asked point blank on the phone to waive a $20 fee, there is nothing you can do to stick to the policy and not come off as a cheapskate. But you will also know that they will be a problem guest if they do this.

Here are our current rates for early check-in:

1-2 bedroom properties: $20 per hour

3-4 bedroom properties: $25 per hour

5+ bedroom properties: $30 per hour

All these fees are rounded to the nearest hour, and we eat the taxes on them. If a guest checks in at 3:40, we are not going to bill them. We are pretty generous with our rounding as well, because it gives us a little bonus in the eyes of the guests. If they message us at 3:20 saying they checked in, we will tell them thanks for letting us know and that it is close enough to normal check-in that we are waiving the fee. Since we are splitting the fee with our property owners and eating taxes on it, it's not worth it for anyone to risk coming across cheap to the guest and start off on the wrong foot to make a few dollars. You are not going to get rich on early check-in fees; the main goal of it is to prohibit every guest from trying to check in early and give your cleaners and maintenance people enough time to do their jobs well. It is also very helpful to have a fee that you can waive if something doesn't go well. If you have a maintenance issue or a complaint, it is nice to have an early check-in or late check-out fee you can waive to make the guest happy. If there is no fee for early check-in or late checkout, then the guest doesn't perceive any financial compensation for the extended time.

Now on to late check-outs. Late check-outs have most of the same difficulties, with a few differences. We do not get as many late check-out requests as early check-in requests; probably about half as many. Late check-out can be a good thing in the slow season, when you are only getting weekend bookings and have all week to work on the rental and get things cleaned. It can be a little bit of extra income when you need it the most.

We still can't technically promise a late check-out until 11:00 the day before the guests checkout, as we could still get a last-minute booking and have a same-day turn. Most of the late check-out issues involve it either being unavailable due to a same-day turn or guests requesting it at the last minute. I often get the request late at night, the night before check-out, or even the morning of, about an hour or two before checkout, when the guest is running behind. I am not going to text the cleaning staff at 11 p.m. and request a late checkout; as the host, it is my job to be on duty 24 hours a day, but it is not theirs to be making calendar adjustments late at night. So if the request comes in super late, it's an automatic no in order to preserve our relationship with the cleaners.

This can lead to some annoyance for the guest and risk leaving them with a bad taste in their mouth, so approve late check-outs as often as possible and take the time to give a good explanation when you cannot do so.

If you get a last-second late checkout request, there is nothing you can really do but tell the guests no and give the cleaners a heads up that the guests may be checking out late without permission, so they can choose to head to a different home first if possible. Guests consistently check out late after being told no, and also without any warning or asking permission. We have a sign by the front door of every unit that says in bold print, "Check-out time is at 10:00. The cleaning staff will show up between 10:00 and 10:15." As a culture, people don't really care about rules, and because most OTA guests have the buffer of the review process, they know you can't be really pushy and rude even if they are late. If you try to charge them a fee, they will give you a bad review. So be as firm as you can be politely, and don't bother showing up until 10:30 or so because people will not be out on time.

One tip to help with flexibility on same-day turns is to post on the check-out sign the cleaner's phone number to text when checking out, assuming that your cleaner is fine with this. Often guests do check out early to catch a flight or start a long drive, and if they check out three or four hours early and let the cleaners know, the cleaners have a lot more flexibility in their schedule. Sometimes having the cleaner's number posted can backfire on the cleaners a bit, with guests texting them instead of management about items left behind or feedback about the property. Our cleaners are team players and don't complain about this, but you need to be aware that guests are random and will probably tell the cleaners about the leaky faucet instead of you.

It's also fairly common for the person who has booked the party to leave the property on time, but other people in their party to be dragging their feet and check out late, so any communication asking them to leave and you communicating that back to the cleaner becomes a three- or four-way communication, with a lag time with each message. For example, the cleaner shows up at 10:15, and there are still cars in the driveway. The cleaner texts the head cleaner, who texts us; we text the guest; the guest texts the person who was last to check out; and then the response works its way all the way back in the chain. Cleaners need to be patient and professional people. You can't have someone going and banging on the door and giving the guest an earful. We have also had bizarre situations with late check-outs. Once, a blind lady got left behind by the party she booked, couldn't get a hold of an Uber to get a ride, and then fell asleep in the master bedroom. With no car in the driveway to let the cleaner know someone was still in the house, she walked in to hear the sound of someone snoring and proceeded to flee the premises while calling me and asking what the heck was going on. Such are the bizarre interactions when dealing with humans, and no matter how good your policies are, there are anomalies. Sometimes tired, blind people get left behind.

Now let's move on to another important policy to determine: your cancellation policy. The policy you choose is critical to acquiring the type of guests that you want as well as determining how your calendar fills up. In general, we err on the strict side when it comes to selecting the cancellation policy, but we have loosened up a bit on some platforms to compete with the decreased demand in the current market. If everyone else in your market is offering free cancellations up to seven days out, you really can't hold to a strict, 60 day out policy.

Generally speaking, if you have a flexible cancellation policy, you will attract guests that want or "need" a flexible cancellation policy. You will even get guests who will book other properties besides yours and then decide later which ones they want to cancel and which one they feel like keeping. There are too many variables that could cause guests to cancel to roll the dice on not receiving any payment upon cancellation.

Here are some common reasons we encounter for cancellations:

- Financial Hardship.
- Wedding cancellation or event cancellation.
- I booked a get together and some of the members can't make it.
- I can't get off work or get called into work.
- Travel dates need to change.
- Health concern of the person who booked or anyone in their family.
- Inclement weather makes it unsafe to travel.
- Rain is forecasted for their dates.
- The car broke down and was in the shop.
- There was no actual reason; they just changed their minds.

Airbnb is constantly changing their options for cancellation policies, and which one you should choose is dependent upon your market and risk tolerance, but ours is usually the strictest or second strictest policy, wherein guests are not eligible for a refund if they cancel less than 60 days from their stay. In our market, especially with our larger cabins, many bookings occur more than 60 days out, and we are dropping our price significantly within the 60-day time frame.

For all the other OTA's, we are the payment processor, and many of our cabins are under a policy that offers a full refund minus a fixed fee, usually around $150, if they cancel up to 60 days from the stay. We still lose the credit card processing fees when refunding the guest, so we need some incentive to keep guests from booking a property and then canceling just prior to the 60-day mark. Let's go over a few issues caused by cancellations, and then we will go over some pushback given by guests who cancel and don't get a refund.

Cancellations often lead to weird available dates on the calendar and mess with how the dates surrounding that booking are filled. We don't put restrictions on check-in and check-out days, only on the minimum number of nights. We will get into this in detail in the next chapter, but typically, anyone who books far out is paying a premium and should get to choose their dates. So let's say a traveler chooses an uncommon travel date, for example, Wednesday night through Saturday morning.

Once two weekend dates are booked, our software drops the price and minimum stay for the remaining days between those dates. Not many people want to check in on a Saturday night; Thursday and Friday are much more common. So after you receive this strange booking, the price drops on Saturday night, and you pick up a one-night stay. If your traveler who booked the strange dates cancels, you are left with a jammed-up weekend with a Saturday night only at a low rate, which is why you better be able to keep at least some of the money from that cancellation. You are not likely to find another traveler who wants to check out on a Saturday morning without lowering your rates significantly.

Cancellations that lead to filling the calendar at the last minute also lead to lower-quality guests because of the lower price point, and they can also increase the risk of damages or a poor rating because of the lower-quality guests or a potential Friday night party.

Now let's move on to guest pushbacks on cancellation requests. Notice I said cancellation requests, not cancellations. Oftentimes, we get guests who say they absolutely have to cancel and cannot keep their reservation and ask for an exception to the cancellation policy. When we politely refuse to make an exception and they realize they are not getting their money back, somehow they are magically able to make the trip. It's amazing how not being able to get a refund magically gets them off work or makes Grandma's funeral dates change.

However, this is not ideal and may be the toughest variable in the cancellation issue. If you reject a refund request, you upset the traveler, and if they show up ticked off at you, expect them to be demanding and unrealistic in their expectations. If one small thing goes wrong, they will give you a bad review because of it (even if they never told you about it during the stay or gave you a chance to correct it). This vindictive mindset is very difficult to overcome. For this reason, if someone is fishing for a refund and is showing signs of being a super disagreeable person, and you believe you can fill the dates of the stay, consider going ahead and refunding them and getting them out of your life. Many travelers will tip their hand as to whether they will actually cancel or not depending on whether you will refund them; with enough experience, you can often guess if they actually will or will not cancel if they don't get the refund. But you can still be very wrong. Some variables to consider when deciding to make an exception are:

- Likelihood of filling the dates, and at what price.
- How much has the property been earning recently, and how much income is needed?
- Length of guest stay, and if you can fill the same number of nights.
- Likelihood of the guest showing up anyway and giving you a bad review.
- Likelihood of the guest postponing their cancellation until the last second, or just before their next payment is due, and if you will be able to book at that point.
- How many reviews do you have, what is the review score of the property, and how much of a bad rating will hurt you?

At the end of the day, experience will go a long way, but it is still a roll of the dice. We tend to be more firm, treat our business like a business, and roll with the punches. It is not wrong to be more flexible, but we have a duty to our owners to make them as much money as possible while taking a long-term perspective of their listings health and review score.

There are a myriad of other complications and pushbacks that you will get with cancellations. First, people often don't read the cancellation policy, and even if they do read it, they don't understand it. For example, most guests miss that a 50% "refund" is them not having to pay the second payment; they actually won't get any money back; their card just won't be charged for the second payment that they owe. Airbnb also doesn't make it clearest that they will not refund the significant Airbnb service fee that they charge, and they are only receiving a "refund" of 50% of the rent, not the Airbnb fee or the large amount of taxes collected by Airbnb for the reservation. Guests often try to show us the math and demand more money back, not understanding that Airbnb is keeping their service fee and not understanding that we are not the payment processor and don't have their money. Airbnb doesn't pay out any money to the host until the time of the guest's stay, so we literally do not have a dime of their money, yet we get accused of unjustly withholding a refund they think they are due.

It does not help that Airbnb has rather poor customer service, and if the traveler calls for an explanation or charges, after an hour on hold they will likely get someone who can't speak English and either doesn't understand the charges or how the refund works, or intentionally won't admit to the guest that they will not be getting back the Airbnb service fee or sales tax. Airbnb typically refunds the cleaning fee if the guest cancels before check-in. Airbnb will not refund their service fee or taxes unless the host agrees to a full refund. All this adds up to a rather complicated math problem that does not add up to an even 50% "refund" to the guest and will result in a whole lot of questions and an upset traveler.

Now let's say you make a decision to approve a partial or additional refund that is not a full refund. Sometimes you can incentivize a difficult traveler to cancel if you give them a partial refund. Even if they don't take the deal of a partial refund, just offering makes you come across as a bit nicer as someone who tried to meet in the middle and puts the guest in a better mood if they decide to come. If you offer a partial refund as an exception and they agree to it, it triggers a clunky process for accomplishing that. You have to work with Airbnb support to get them refunded any amount other than a full refund, which usually involves multiple phone calls or messages with Airbnb.

If the guest cancels and is not eligible for a refund, they will often continue to send you messages asking for a refund and contacting Airbnb for help. Airbnb likes to show guests how traveler-friendly they are and will call you and message you multiple times on behalf of the guest, even after you have clearly stated that you will not approve a refund. Likely, you will get a call from someone at 10:30 at night from someone who can't speak English trying to get a guest a refund.

It is fairly common for guests to try to negotiate a refund if they cancel, and you are able to rebook the dates. This is a tricky one to get out of, but it is not a game that I play. Once I successfully get an angry guest to cancel, I consider the transaction closed. I don't want to deal with them asking me what rate I rebooked at, how much they will get refunded, and on and on and on. When a transaction is done, let it be done. You also need this money to balance out the times you get canceled and can't get rebooked.

Sometimes, in lieu of canceling, they want to move the dates. A deceitful guest may be trying to get you to move the dates far enough out that they are eligible for free cancellation again. We rarely agree to move dates further back, for several reasons that are hard to get the guests to understand. First of all, they usually are moving dates that are in the relatively near future and have little chance of rebooking at a good rate to a far-out date that is likely to book at a good rate. If you approve that change of date, it will cost you money. Sometimes guests want credit for a future stay at some vague date. This is also a no-no. If you can't rebook their dates for at least the price they booked for, you are losing money, and having to work with Airbnb support to give them credit for some future stay is a nightmare compounded. If you are foolish enough to approve a credit for a future stay, which I have done once or twice, you can make it for a smaller amount that must be used within a certain time frame. For example, if they are canceling a $1,000 booking, give them a $500 credit to be used in the next 6 months. It is not ideal, but it can work in specific situations to reward a guest to actually cancel and stop the drama.

Another guest trick that might trip you up with a flexible cancellation policy is a guest canceling and immediately rebooking at a lower rate. If you have pricing software that will drop rates at the last minute with no cancellation penalty to keep them from playing games, it is tough to avoid this.

Another variation of canceling is reducing the number of days in their stay. If their stay is far enough out and we are likely to get that date booked, we will often approve it. It also depends on how long they have been booked for when they request it. If they just booked yesterday for six months out and they want to reduce from six nights to five nights, you are going to come across as a bad host if you deny that, sour your relationship with the guest, and risk a bad review. However, if the dates are not far out and they have jammed up your calendar for a while by having those dates blocked off, you need to figure out a way to politely tell them they have to keep the reservation they have made. This does not apply to extra pet fees or extra guest fees; we allow guests to alter those and receive a refund as needed.

It is possible that a guest who doesn't like the no refund policy will charge back their credit card and win the credit card dispute. We get a handful of chargebacks a year and I'd say we win about 60% of them. Ultimately, it is up to the bank, and despite providing a very clear rental agreement with a clearly laid out cancellation policy, sometimes the banks will side with their client and issue them a refund.

When dealing with guests attempting to negotiate a cancellation deal, it is important to assess if there are other parties at play. Oftentimes, on our large cabins, we will have multiple families splitting the costs of the rental, and so all parties involved have to approve of the cancellation decision and settlement. Often the relative of the booking guest who paid for half of the reservation is ticked off because they didn't know about or don't understand the cancellation policy, and there is a lot of drama flaring up behind the scenes that you can't see.

Over the years, I have compiled a profile of guests who will be trouble, especially around cancellations. I hope this will help you in your decision-making about how to deal with them and at what point it is worth taking the financial hit of getting them off of your calendar.

Troubled guests will call you. Most interaction with guests is through the messaging app of the

OTA, which is how it should be. If a guest calls you angry, know that they are at significant risk of being that type of guest that will ruin your day. They are not content to send a message or an email; they want to aggressively push you for a refund on the phone. Troubled guests also have their relatives reach out to you. If you get a call from the mother of the booking guest or a question in the form of a new inquiry by a relative of the booking guest, it is a sign of trouble. There is a lot of miscommunication and misinformation in the family, and they will be trouble.

Troubled guests don't read or don't understand the policies, and they often ask questions in an incoherent way that makes them difficult to answer. Troubled guests refuse to look up anything for themselves and will ask for information that is simple to look up on Google.

Troubled guests will have a volume of questions before their stay. If they have a volume of questions before their stay, they will likely have a volume of questions and complaints during their stay. These guests will be aggressive, not tactful or polite, but will violate social norms in escalating situations.

Cancellation requests are stressful, but for the most part, when they are done, they are done. If you are a DIY host, there is little recourse that a guest can take if they don't receive a refund. This is a huge advantage to not being a business with a public image that can be threatened and targeted. Yes, the traveler who booked your property has your phone number from Airbnb, and they can call and text you, but that is about the extent of the exposure. If they are really motivated and have your rental property address, they may be able to locate your full name and personal address, but that's unlikely, and most people won't stoop to that level of crazy.

Let me summarize this section on cancellations by telling a rather painful story that pulls together a lot of the cancellation variables we have covered.

We had a reservation canceled by a guest, a Christmas booking from an out-of-state traveler. She stated that their group could no longer travel due to her mom's cancer. We hear this story quite often, and although it is unfortunate to be the cold-hearted business owner, we told her we could not approve a refund. Large groups that book 9 months in advance very often have one or two members that end up not being able to travel, and you cannot make exceptions for every exception request you get.

We asked if she had purchased Travelers Insurance, which we also sell and encourage our travelers to purchase in case there is an illness. Of course they had not, and she began to be a bit aggressive in her messaging with me, asking if they could receive a refund if the dates were rebooked. I informed her we would not do that. She went ahead and canceled during Airbnb's "50%" refund window, according to the cancellation policy.

A couple months after she canceled, we did get the dates rebooked, though at a lower price. I got a call from the sister of the woman who had booked, who did not identify herself, but asked if those Christmas dates were available. They had been watching the calendar to see if it would rebook, and once I confirmed that they were not available, she identified herself and demanded a refund. She got very nasty on the phone with me, and after an uncomfortable conversation, I foolishly thought it was over.

Her sister sent up a follow-up message on Airbnb, confirming that I had told them over the phone I would not be issuing a refund. I politely confirmed that was the case.

The cyber bullying attack started that night. The sister of the woman who booked posted the sob story on Facebook and posted our phone number and Google profile, encouraging all her Facebook friends to give us a bad review and to call and let me know what they think. I was already asleep at about 10 p.m. when I got the first threatening phone call. Then my phone started buzzing with notifications from our Google account about one-star reviews. Up until that point, we only had about 30 reviews on Google and a perfect 5-star rating from guests who had stayed with us. Now that began to plummet.

My administrative manager located the sister's post on Facebook and notified me of what she had done. I called the sister who had made the post and tried to get her to get her friends to stop harassing us. The phone call did not go well, but I did make an audio recording of it and got her to directly state she would get all her friends to stop and remove the reviews if we refunded her the money.

I am not the type to be bullied, so of course I never complied. The drama went on for several days. I got calls from all sorts of interesting people, like one man who said he had friends in high places in the media, and I gave me a deadline to refund them, or he would make a huge story about our company. He was literally screaming at me on the phone and would not give me a chance to explain the cancellation policy or anything else. The posts on Google and our company Facebook page continued, including personal attacks on me, accusations of me cursing out the guests on the phone, and other unfounded accusations.

My mistakes in the situation were plenty; not that I did anything wrong or actually withheld any money, but that I did not actually hone in on the core issues and address them. They were so angry and belligerent, and I was so stressed that I didn't understand that they thought they were due a refund; I thought they were just upset that I hadn't made an exception and approved a full refund. They were also STR hosts, and I assumed they actually knew how Airbnb worked. Somehow they thought I had received their money, and I was refusing to refund them according to the policy. Once I realized this, I explained that this was not true and not possible, since Airbnb held the money and refunded it according to policy. They didn't realize that the 50% refund they were owed was actually not making the second payment, and they would not receive any money back from their initial payment.

Of course, I got no support from Airbnb; I could not get the guest to speak with anyone from Airbnb who could explain things, and so they continued to assume I was being dishonest. They continued to text me and send nasty messages, but at last I stopped trying to explain the cancellation policy that they either did not want to or literally could not understand, and I asked them not to contact me anymore.

After about five or six days, things cooled off. We reported the reviews to Google, since only people who have had an experience with your business are supposed to be able to leave a review on your profile. However, you can't call or get a hold of anyone at Google, so when you report a review, if Google's algorithm doesn't flag that review as illegitimate, it won't remove it. Some of the reviews had keywords that were easy to flag, like "my friend booked a home," which clearly showed they didn't do business with us, and some had profanity and could be removed. We are currently down to only five one-star reviews from the cyber bullying attack, so I guess all in all, it could have been worse.

I hope you never experience something that extreme. I tell the story so that you can see what happens when guests don't understand the cancellation policy and also the extent of the drama that guests can create if things don't go their way.

Let's conclude this part on cancellations on a positive note, about when things go right with cancellations. Sometimes guests actually understand your policy and have to cancel anyway, and they just voluntarily cancel without any drama. Sometimes they even send you a friendly note, something to the effect of "The wedding got canceled. I'm sorry that we can't stay at your beautiful cabin. I understand we will lose our deposit, but I hope we can come again sometime."

Celebrating a little extra income is not greedy. We have one property that seems to get a lot of cancellations, and we make about $3,000 a year on cancellations.

Remember, cancellation income is necessary to offset losses from decreased prices on rebooking and getting stuck with awkward or vacant dates.

Figure out what policy works in your market and stick to it, unless your gut and experience tell you otherwise.

Property Damage:

Property damage is not as common as most new STR owners think it is. This is a common question (and rightfully so) from new property owners, but small, accidental damage only occurs about 1-3% of the time in our rentals. When it does occur, it can generate a tricky situation, not only in regards to collecting payment, but in regards to avoiding a bad review.

Let's run through some common occurrences and their outcomes. Some guests accidentally break a wine glass or lamp, and will notify you about it, apologize, and offer to pay for it. If you have the right type of property and are attracting the right type of guests, you generally have people who will fess up and offer restitution. We had one gentleman who fell at night, and grabbed a decorative toilet paper holder on the way down and broke it. It was not a common in-stock item from Walmart, but this guest had the decency to not only notify us and take responsibility, but even located the exact same item on Ebay while he was still on the trip and ordered it for us.

There are also people who will break things, and tell you after they check out, or just admit to it once you ask about it. We have had a guest break an end table and then put it by the front door with no explanation. They were clearly not trying to get away with it, but for some reason didn't tell us.

And then there are the troubled guests, who won't take responsibility for their party. My theory is that most non-reported damage that occurs is not told to the booking guest, and the guest that you are actually communicating with honestly didn't know about it. Little Johnny doesn't tell Aunt Suzy that he tried to do a pull-up on the blinds and broke them. If Suzy doesn't happen to go into Johnny's room before checkout, or if Johnny is a little older and more deceptive and can manipulate the blinds into looking normal, then no responsible adult is aware of the situation.

When you report this type of damage back to the guest, they say there is no way their party could have done such a thing. Not only do they deny it, but they get up on their high horse and tell you how much integrity they have and how they always leave a place better than they found it, and there is no way they will pay this audacious charge.

You must be careful in your wording, and use your best judgment on if and when to bill a guest. If you are operating your property effectively, you have the margin to forgive a few $10-20 broken items per year, and not risk getting bad reviews for trying to collect on those damages that don't move the needle.

Let's take a look at some options you have on different platforms as far as damage is concerned.

Airbnb requires you to request money from the guest through the resolution center, and only if the guest denies the charge will they step in and get involved. When we do get damages covered, it is always unclear if Airbnb is paying it out of pocket or if they end up charging the guest card. Either way, they make you jump through a lot of hoops, as spelled out in chapter two. Make sure you have your cleaners or whoever is first on site, photograph the damaged item or area as soon as possible, exactly as they found it. Airbnb has loosened up their window for a claim a bit. I think it is now up to two weeks, whereas it used to be before the next guest checked in, which had us rushing resolution requests on same-day turns. Wait a few days and hope that the guest leaves a review before requesting money. Just remember, the guest can edit their review until you leave yours, so wait till they review you, and then review them to lock in their review. You don't have to give them a bad review just because they accidentally damaged something; you just don't want them to alter it to a negative review once you send them the bill.

If the booking is through Vrbo, and they have purchased a Generali policy, you will have to submit all the documentation for a claim. Last time we did one, it wasn't all that hard, but was quite annoying. I find all the paperwork annoying, though, so I could be jaded. If they didn't buy insurance and you can withhold their damage deposit or charge their card, make sure you send a detailed explanation of the damage and itemize the charge. When we are charging for damage, we usually charge immediately before sending them a message, so they don't block or change their credit card information before the charge goes through.

I have a couple of other minor items that are a bit tough that I want to cover briefly. The first is how and when to notify a guest of a potential issue. When unplanned things happen, like an appliance going down, the heat going out, or even a major amenity breaking, you need to let the guest know before check-in to set realistic expectations. You should know that Airbnb will consider any significant amenity as grounds for giving a full refund, but you do still want the guest to know in advance, because the guest canceling and getting a refund is not the worst case scenario for you. The worst case scenario is them checking in, complaining all weekend, then leaving a critical review, and then getting a full refund from Airbnb, including the cleaning fee that you still have to pay the cleaners for. Sometimes people are traveling from far away, and are already on the road or on their flight, but telling them is the right thing to do and is best for you as well.

The tougher part is when you think you will have a solution before they check in. If you have an appliance repair scheduled the morning of their stay, or the day before, do you tell them? Some guests get very anxious at the idea of something not working during their stay, so in my opinion it is better to keep them in the dark if there is a very high probability of a satisfactory resolution before their stay. Just try to get a realistic appraisal of the odds of success before making that decision. If they don't find out until 30 minutes before the internet is out, they will be very upset that they didn't have a chance to find another accommodation, and will bring that attitude into the reservation.

Another similar tricky one is giving guests advanced warning about inclement weather, especially if your driveway or road is not suitable for snow or ice. Many guests are concerned and will track weather, and if there is a predicted storm, they may want to cancel in advance and want a refund. We do not allow this too far in advance, and will only allow them to cancel for a refund about 24-48 hours out if there is a high likelihood of a bad storm and power outage, and if the home does not have a backup generator, or has an access road that is steep and can cause them to be stuck at the property.

At the end of the day you will be able to successfully resolve most situations with good communication and patience. The only really tough situation comes when you get someone who is just an irrational, angry person who happens to be the one in a hundred reservations that has a fluke event like no heat during a cold snap. A tough guest with a tough issue is the perfect storm, and it will take you on your A-game to come out of it without having to visit your therapist.

CHAPTER 7

PETS, POLICIES & PRICING

The decision to be pet friendly or not is probably the most debated question among short-term rental hosts. Allowing travelers to bring pets causes a good bit of work and some risk, and the decision ultimately comes down to the host's risk tolerance and willingness to put in extra work.

Before we get too far into it, let's define "pet". Typically the pet is a dog, but occasionally we do get requests for cats or other even more non-common traveling companions. Our request to bring a non-canine is less than 1% a year of all pet requests, so if you are worried about cat allergies or cat spraying in the house, it is not going to hurt you to restrict cats.

More and more people have "fur babies," and more and more of these pet owners are traveling with their pets. I suppose it was a COVID thing for everyone to go out and get a dog, or two, or three. When people travel, they likely will have to pay for a pet sitter, pay to drop their dog at a kennel, or will pay to take their pet with them. We encourage our owners to be pet friendly, but do not push them to change their mind if they are not inclined to be. Having a pet friendly space certainly increases both occupancy and rates, though it is difficult to ascertain by how much. The only black and white financial metric you get is from pet fees collected, which among most of our homes is about 2,000 to $3,000 per year, depending on the occupancy that the home is doing. I am positive that being pet friendly also increases occupancy, as many of our post traveler survey respondents said that being pet friendly was one of the primary reasons why they booked our listing and not somewhere else.

Yes, dogs can be destructive. But so can kids and you can't outlaw them. Come to think of it, kids are more destructive in our experience, but at the end of the day you just need to set up your space as durable as possible for pets and kids. Don't have a fabric couch that can absorb and retain dog odor. Yes, you can have a no pets on the couch rule, but good luck enforcing it. If you're going to be pet friendly, you really want to avoid carpet, which you should be doing anyway.

Being pet friendly is a lot of work, and is almost as much customer service work as the early check-in and late check-out requests that we get. Many times, guests don't know who in their group will be bringing pets, and so they are asking about your policy, and then talking to their group, and may or may not be adding pets to their reservation closer to their stay. As a host, you must follow up with the guests who imply they may be bringing pets but then don't get back to you. No OTAs handle pet fees well, as they don't allow for tiered pet rates or multiple pet fees for a guest. This means that you will have to manually collect payment for pet fees and refund any canceled pet fees. This also means that to do things right, you must properly collect and remit the taxes, since Airbnb doesn't pay taxes on fees collected through the resolution center.

Our pet fees are scaled based on how expensive the property is and whether or not the property has any pet specific amenities like a fenced-in yard. Many of our listings have a fenced in space for pets, and dog owners will certainly pay more for having a fenced yard. In our surveys we send out after checkout, 23% of guests say they would pay $10 a night for a fenced yard; 19% said they would pay $20 a night, and 18% said they would pay $30 a night for fenced in pets. Yes, that leaves 40% saying they would not pay, but this is a survey sent to all groups, not just ones that brought a dog, which means that essentially all travelers with pets and even some that do would pay more for a fenced yard.

Right now we have three tiers of pet fees: $60, $85, and $100. You can also have a pet fee per night, which is a little bit more complicated strategy, but can help you avoid taking a long booking for a low pet fee. We do this on a few of our nicer listings and charge an additional $20 per night after the first three nights. Remember that the guest will be charged taxes on top of these fees, so this will add up to a significant amount of money for the guest.

When determining a fee, you will, as always, want to conduct some market research and see how many listings in your area are pet friendly, and what they are charging. Our smaller cabins churn out more pet fees than our large properties, even though the large properties obviously have a higher number of guests. Most likely, this is due to higher occupancy rates, and also because larger groups are flying in from far away for weddings and family reunions and decide to leave their dog at home, whereas the smaller cabins are primarily small families and couples getaways that are driving up from the Atlanta area and bringing Fido with them. AirDNA has some pretty quick stats where you can pull how many units are pet friendly, or you can just enter the pet friendly search filter in Airbnb or Vrbo and do the math to calculate the percentage of listings that are pet friendly. Our market used to be only about 33% pet friendly, but now we are just under 50% of listings being pet friendly.

Additional cleaning is one of the bigger considerations to make when deciding on whether to be pet friendly or not. Your cleaners will have to contend with dog hair, which will get stuck on everything. Cleaners may not directly charge more for cleaning pet friendly homes, but you should disclose whether or not you will be pet friendly when getting a quote from a cleaner. You will need to change your HVAC filters more frequently, and will need to monitor the yard for treats left behind when people don't clean up after their dogs. But for the most part, most dog owners are responsible and clean after themselves, and dogs are usually a non-issue.

One of the more difficult aspects of pet fees is the growing number of travelers that have emotional support animals, or ESA's. As this has become more common culturally, many travelers now expect you to waive the pet fee if they have an ESA, but you are not required to, and I would encourage you not to. We do get some pushback from travelers who say that other hosts have waived the pet fee for their ESA, and complain if we hold our ground. This is how hosts enter into this feedback loop of giving more and more things away that they should rightfully be able to charge for. An ESA is not a service animal, and its owners should not be given the same advantages as those with specially trained animals that are trained to perform specific tasks and help them function. Of course, this is my opinion, and likely many bleeding hearts will just waive the fee for anyone who asks, but I believe that it does a disservice to those who have a legitimate disability and have jumped through the hoops to have a service animal.

A host should never try to charge for a service animal, or request documentation for a service animal, as these are both illegal and a great way to get a terrible review. It is hard to determine how many people take advantage of the lack of proof required to have a service animal, but since this service animal request is not that frequent, I don't think it's too widely abused. The following is from ADA.gov:

"If you are working at a business or state/local government facility and it is unclear to you whether someone's dog is a service dog, you may ask for certain information using two questions." You may ask:

Is the dog a service animal required because of a disability? What work or task has the dog been trained to perform?

You are not allowed to:

Request any documentation that the dog is registered, licensed, or certified as a service animal.

Require that the dog demonstrate its task, or inquire about the nature of the person's disability.

We don't go so far as to ask any questions from the guest because they aren't required to prove anything, and it just makes you look bad. If you do ask for clarification, don't stray from the approved questions.

If you decide to be pet-friendly, you may decide to have rules for pets in your space. The few rules we post are very reasonable but are probably marginally helpful. For example, you may require a dog to be crated if it is left unattended, but most dog travelers simply will not travel with a crate, and you have no way of knowing if they will comply. Fortunately, most dog owners are responsible, and most will take their dog with them when they go out, which is what this rule may encourage, but again, it is hard to say if it moves the needle.

A few other common rules are:

- No pets on furniture.
- No pets off a leash or unattended outside, even if there is a fenced-in yard.
- No excessive barking.
- All pet feces must be cleaned up.
- All pet hair must be vacuumed up, or an extra cleaning fee will apply.

Do what you can with these rules, or any other ones you may feel necessary, to reduce your liability, but at the end of the day, you have to accept that being pet-friendly poses some additional risk and work, and that is why you charge the fee and pay your cleaners well.

One last consideration in deciding whether or not to be pet-friendly is that it simply makes guests happy. At the end of the day, we are in the make-people-happy business. When people can bring the pets they love with them, they are in a better place and more likely to leave a favorable review. You would be surprised at how many dog owners, who paid a sizable pet fee, sent us private feedback or left a public review about how appreciative they were to be able to bring their pet.

Policies and Rules:

Now let's cover some policies that you should have for your rental to help govern the space, attract the right type of guests, and ward off the wrong type of guests. If you have well-laid, reasonable rules, this does not scare off the best guests on each platform. Most people understand that hosts have to have policies in place to protect their property. Well-laid-out policies also let those looking to party know that you are experienced and prepared to deal with any shenanigans, and they will not be getting away with anything. It is my theory that if your rules and policies are clear and are read by the guest, they just might pop up in the mind of a guest that is tempted to not get their butt in gear to get out by checkout time, or might not have planned to party, but have a few rowdy friends that just might play music a little past the 10:00 quiet hour if they aren't reigned in. What I'm trying to say is that not many guests go into a rental with bad intent, but clear policies help keep those who aren't always the most responsible and considerate of others in check.

The other critical reason to have very specific rules is that they give you legal enforcement of any fees you need to charge or action you need to take for misbehavior. If you do not have a late checkout fee listed in the house rules, Airbnb will not force the guest to pay anything. Every once in a while, you will get a guest that will oversleep and leave hours late, which could even cause you to not have the home ready for the next guest, which you have to reimburse. You must cover your butt by having the ability to charge them, or you will lose money after doing a significant amount of stressful work and possibly getting a bad review from the next guest who couldn't check in on time.

Stuff happens in this business, and a lot of it is just accidental human error. We had one guest think she booked different days than she actually booked, so she showed up a day late, and then at 10:00 on checkout morning, she was hiking on top of a mountain an hour away because she thought she had another night on her trip. There are a lot of things you can't plan for or predict, but your policies help you make the best of bad situations.

One rule that we have that we don't put in our listing is our shipping policy. We don't put it in our listings because it doesn't make us come across as very friendly, it would make our listings longer, and it's not something that is necessary for a guest to know before their trip. But in the information binder on site, in the digital guidebook, and posted in bold print by the front door, we have the following: Please check that you have not left any items behind. Due to the number of items left behind, all items that are requested to be mailed will incur a $30 fee on top of the cost to ship the item.

This rule has helped us out a ton, as it has reduced the number of items we are requested to mail and has compensated us for our time spent going to the post office and mailing items. Somewhat surprisingly, we don't get complaints about the fee on top of the shipping charge. Even with this reminder posted in three places, guests leave stuff behind all the time. Many of them want to drive back and get what they forgot, or come meet you somewhere so they don't have to pay shipping costs or wait for it to be shipped. How you deal with that is up to you; just make sure you are not making your cleaners or next guests uncomfortable. We typically don't allow post-checkout guests to come back or meet up with them due to "safety concerns."

If you are going to mail something for a guest, whether or not you are going to charge an additional fee, make sure you collect payment up front and then mail the item. I think it was my very first time mailing a package for someone that I didn't do this, and I never got reimbursed for the shipping cost. We typically charge more than we expect to have to pay, usually $100, and then we'll refund the guest any additional money after taking out our $30 shipping fee. Make sure you ask them in writing if they want the package insured to reduce liability.

All the other rules we have are laid out in the listing. There may be one or two additional ones that apply to your specific home or that you insist on, but don't make your list of rules too long, or people will not want to book because they will feel like they are back in Catholic school rather than going on vacation. We have some version of this policy posted in each listing on Airbnb. Every channel is different, and you will have to modify your copy or change how it is displayed.

No music, loud noise, or sound-amplifying equipment outside between the hours of 10:00 p.m. and 8:00 a.m.

No pets without a pet fee. The only pets that are allowed are dogs, up to a maximum of two. If it is found that guests brought a pet or pets without disclosing them, the guest will be subject to a $150 fee on top of the pet fees for the number of pets brought.

Guests causing excessive noise or disturbances, including, but not limited to, underage drinking, partying, drug use, and exceeding max occupancy, will be asked to check out immediately, and a full stay rent charge will be due, including the deposit amount, with no refunds.

Guests who leave the place excessively dirty will be subject to an additional cleaning fee. Examples of excessively dirty are stains on the floors and walls, pots and pans left unwashed in the sink, and trash left on the floor and outside.

Any guest that enters the property early without written permission may result in a $50 per hour fee.

Any checkout after 10:00 a.m. without written permission may result in a $50 fee per hour. Anything after 11:00 a.m. is considered 2 hours. Any checkout after 12:00 pm will result in a fee for the entire daily rate, without any discounts, and guests will still not have rights to the property.

Additional requests:

Return all furniture and items to their original locations. Ensure that no dirty dishes are left out and that the dishwasher has been run. If you use up a propane tank, please place it by the front step so we know to refill it.

Quiet hours

10:00 p.m.–8:00 a.m.

No parties or events.

No commercial photography.

A few thoughts on the rules listed:

- Smoking: We restrict smoking in the home, obviously, but allow it 25 feet or more from the home. Having smoking completely restricted will probably slightly hurt your listing in total bookings, and will probably not be followed by people anyway. We have yet to have a bad case of cigarette smoking inside the home. We actually have a more common problem of the house smelling like a pot, but this typically goes away after a good air-out.

- Unauthorized early check-in: Guests will routinely arrive early, and you cannot enforce a fee without coming across as rude and jeopardizing your relationship and the review. Fairly often, we get a message about 15 minutes prior to checking in that says, "We're here early; can we go in?" You will not be able to tell them no or charge them a fee at that point; it's just the way things work. The warning that is listed in the house rules is to prevent people from intentionally showing up hours early and to allow you to charge for your scheduled early check-in. Yes, you can get clever and set your code to only allow a specific guest code right at check-in time, but if your lock has a malfunction or if the guest arrives 5 minutes early and can't get in, they may be frustrated.

- Unauthorized late check-out: Similar to early check-in, late check-out is very, very common. We don't generally enforce the late checkout fee unless it is an egregious late check-out. You do want to make sure that your staff who are first on site immediately notify management that the guests are still not out, as this could hint at an additional issue, such as a party that slept late or guests thinking they booked different dates and don't have to leave. As soon as the cleaners contact us about someone still being on site after check-out, we contact them immediately and fairly aggressively. I will message them through whatever platform they have booked, as well as call them. If it is an Airbnb booking and you can't get a hold of the guest and get them to immediately comply, call Airbnb and report them right away so that it is documented that they are still on site. Airbnb will also reach out to the guest, and you will have a much better chance of collecting your late check-out fees and having their review pulled if it is retaliatory.

Make sure you stay on top of guests and get updates from your cleaners until the guest is actually gone. Many times we have gotten the guest who is already 20 minutes late sending us a message saying they are gone when they are not, or they are "leaving now," and they are still there thirty minutes later.

Maximum Guests and Extra Guest Fees:

Most local governments have a maximum number of guests they are allowed to host, which is often based on the number of bedrooms and possibly the available parking. Unless you have a good reason not to, I would encourage you to allow the maximum number of guests you are allowed by law. If you restrict your four-bedroom house to six people to reduce the risk of parties, you are going to really hurt your income and are mostly preventing rule followers from booking. Many people request to bring more than the maximum number of guests, and I'm sure many actually do without asking. We don't monitor cameras and count heads, though we do ask if guests have an accurate guest count when they book a large home for just one or two people. It is pretty common for people to accidentally book with the wrong number of guests. Many times, people don't read our rules and don't know there is a fee for a certain number of guests.

We generally set our extra guest fee to kick in at about two-thirds to three-quarters of maximum occupancy. If we have two bedrooms with a maximum capacity of six, we usually have a small fee for the fifth and sixth guests. A large cabin sleeping 16 usually has a fee for guests 13–16. We do get some complaints about this, but not enough to discourage us from assigning the fee. Usually the complaints are private, usually before an inquiry, and not in a public review. When we do get questions or complaints about it, we don't really have a great answer for the justification, as we pretty much do it because it helps us make more money, and that is what we are in business for. Our explanation is something to the effect that we are trying to keep the cabin more affordable for smaller groups and try to get the larger groups to pay a little more for some of the overhead, like extra supplies and utilities associated with hosting larger groups.

Pricing Software

Pricing is one of the most critical steps to attracting the right type of guests at the right occupancy rates for the current market. With your rates and length of stay set appropriately, you can reduce your risk of lower-quality guests, maximize rents that are realistic to achieve given the demand and season, and achieve a predictable income in future months so you know what type of cash flow you will be working with.

Setting your pricing is a lot like playing The Price is Right game show; you must pick the highest price possible without going too high and not getting a booking.

The trickiest part about pricing is that it is difficult to know where you went wrong. If your property is not booked six months out and you drop the price by 15%, were you slightly overpriced and missed a potential guest that would have booked at a price 10% less? Should you do a very gradual pricing strategy, like drop rates by 2-3 percent per week on far-out reservations, or should you hold fast to your prices and just occasionally do significant discounts to see if you can find a price point people will pay for?

The only real data you have is what comps in your area have on the books for reservations. This is a huge advantage for a management company like ours, which gets a good feel for the market without having to scroll through local listings to see how many bookings they have at different intervals. We do check the market, but we don't have to check it as frequently because we know if our other three bedrooms are booked for the fall already; the ones or two that are not are probably overpriced and need a reduction.

Some pricing software like PriceLabs has a metric that compares your occupancy with the overall market, which is hugely helpful, but I think it is also important to know at what price point those reservations are as well. It is important that you establish some accurate comps in the area and regularly check their pricing and availability. This does not mean that you should panic and drop your price because one of your competitors has, or jack up your price because one of your competitors is really proud of their listing on certain dates. You just need to know how they are pricing and if they are landing bookings or are hearing crickets chirp.

A lot of pricing comes down to experience and a specific customer avatar. Some of our listings do really well in the fall for wedding parties, but once the wedding parties have all made their reservations in the spring, I need to do a significant price drop because most of our other guests will just be regular "leaf lookers" who are looking to book at a lower price point. There is also an avatar of vacationers who plan far in advance and are willing to pay a premium for the dates and location that they want. This is why it pays to keep your prices high in advance. I never understood the strategy of giving discounts to people booking far in advance; these are the travelers who have the highest value for a specific property and are willing to pay for the value they assign.

One of the craziest things about the pricing game is that booking patterns are changing constantly. There are cultural and economic changes that cause travelers to plan farther in advance or book more at the at the last minute. Sometimes we will get a flurry of reservations in late January for summer vacations and weddings; sometimes that flurry doesn't hit until March or April. Some years, we have a more gradual booking rhythm and don't have as many clusters of bookings. All this is to say that you need to monitor the market and can't just say, "Well, I had Thanksgiving and Christmas booked by this time last year, so I must be overpriced." When people book constantly, what they book for rarely changes, so if you build a great net, you will continue to catch enough fish to keep food on the table.

How low you are willing to drop your rate depends on your cost per day for a rented property, your cost per day for a vacant property, and the minimum profit that makes it worth your time to manage and take on the associated risk of a guest stay. We will get into calculating your supply costs and how to think about this later in the book.

As one who values my time, I would not host a guest for a maximum net of $20 or $30. There is always bandwidth and time associated with managing a reservation, so there just has to be more meat on the bone than that for me. Some of our owners have expressed this same sentiment to me, which is a fair consideration. They just don't want to take on a reservation past a certain threshold where they are making peanuts after we take our commission for management and they take on the associated overhead.

Pricing your listing too low sometimes attracts more difficult guests. However, many lower-priced reservations churn out fine guests, and I think sometimes a few bad experiences at a low point make hosts afraid to drop rates at all. When the market is down, dropping your price and having a 25% drop in net profit is far better than not dropping and getting a 30% drop in occupancy and an 80% drop in profit. These are obviously made-up numbers, but I am trying to illustrate that net profit is very sensitive to a drop in revenue, as you obviously have to hit a certain threshold of income to just meet your expenses. Yes, operating at discounted rates may mean you will have to deal with difficult guests, but that's why you have excellent damage policies and systems in place in order to deal with those issues.

Now that we have talked about a few pricing strategies, we need to add the pricing software to the conversation. Using pricing software is a must for time savings and the accuracy of rates. There are several pricing software out there, but not nearly as many as there are PMS. Make sure you select one that connects to all the channels you use or are thinking about using. The largest software companies are currently beyond Pricing, Wheelhouse, and PriceLabs is the software that we have used for years, and we are overall happy with the service. Some software doesn't have a fixed monthly fee but only takes 1% of bookings, which is a horrible business model to subject yourself to.

Pricing software is very far from set-it and forget-it software, and it takes a lot of work to learn and utilize it effectively. Between the work and the additional cost, you may ask if it is worth it, but it definitely is. Most hosts see a large jump in revenue when they begin to use pricing software.

The main reason why it is worth it is because your rates and minimum stay automatically updated with each booking, and your pricing updates constantly based on market factors without you having to monitor and make the adjustments. There are a myriad of options and settings you can set up, but just the basic ones are enough to really make a difference in how competitive and accurate your pricing is. For example, when you get a gap between two bookings, you can create rules where these available "orphan" days automatically get a discount applied to them. So if you get a weekend booked and you already have a reservation the following weekend, you can apply a 15% or 20% discount to the remaining weekdays between the two reservations. Most pricing software refreshes and pushes new rates to the OTA's daily, which would never happen if it wasn't automatic. You also get a boost in SEO from most OTAs when you are consistently updating your pricing, so it is good when your calendar gets updated every day.

Other features that we depend on with PriceLabs are their last-minute discount, which is a percentage discount that begins at a chosen time frame. Every property is different, and you will want to tune up your settings based on the market and your listings' performance, but many of our properties have had around a 50% discount over the last 50 days, so the listing is getting about 1% cheaper per day until it hits our minimum price. There are other factors that affect the overall rate, and the recommended price from the software comes into play, but it is still a great feature that allows you to discount gradually up to your minimum price.

Although I am a fan of PriceLabs and the power of pricing software in general, some of its shortcomings are pretty bad. This year I have found the recommended pricing for our market to be completely inaccurate, which means I have to do manual overrides on the majority of the dates, which is time-consuming. This year, guests are booking much more at the last minute, and we are experiencing lower occupancy rates and daily rates. PriceLabs has been dropping our prices on weekends to crazy low rates in the 21–45 day out window, which is where a lot of our weekends are being booked right now, especially on our small to midsized units. They also have been pushing the maximum price on weekdays about 90 days out or more, which is frustrating. Unless it is the week of Christmas or Thanksgiving, I rarely let my weekday rates float to the maximum price, as it discourages longer stays. When your Sunday night through Thursday night is at an expensive rate; you are not going to get 4–7 night bookings. You might get a Friday and Saturday night booked at a high rate, but expensive weekdays make the overall cost of the reservation too high for most of your travelers and decrease the odds of you getting those advanced bookings.

Another shortcoming PriceLabs has is that it won't drop the price or minimum stay on one weekend day if you get the weekend partially booked. If someone is checking out on a Saturday, you will need to discount Saturday night and drop it to a one-night minimum manually. If someone books to check in on Saturday, you will need to manually edit Friday. I guess that brings up another debated topic, which is whether or not you should restrict which days travelers can check in or check out. It is not ideal when a guest checks out on a Saturday, as it makes it difficult, though not impossible, to get another reservation starting that day. We do not have any restrictions on this, because guests in our market typically want to check in on a Friday and out on either Sunday or Monday anyway, and guests who are seeking non-typical dates are usually either booking far in advance and still paying an overall high price or are booking at the at the last minute, and you are grateful to get something on the books, even if it means someone checking in or out on a Saturday. As long as you have at least a two-night minimum, getting a weird check-in or check-out date shouldn't hurt you. Another issue you may run into if you have multiple properties and have restrictions on days that guests can check in and check out is that you will end up with a high percentage of your listings turning on the same day. If you are using the same cleaning and maintenance people across different listings, it is a good thing when your turnovers are spread out throughout the week. Because of the number of properties we have, we will have at least a handful of turns on irregular days like Saturdays and Tuesdays, which is not a bad thing for scheduling. If we thought we would increase revenue by restricting days, I would, but it would make operations much more difficult. People getting into the industry don't quite understand how difficult it is to find good staff for cleanings and repairs on multiple same-day turns that hit on the same day.

Another common mistake I see is hosts not making extreme enough seasonal adjustments. Usually this manifests itself by not going cheap enough in the slow season, but occasionally I see underpricing during the during the peak season. Around here, if you do not have a killer listing with a hot tub, you are not going to get anywhere near your maximum rate, even on weekends in January and February. You might as well keep them discounted a year to eighteen months out and compete for those few travelers that are booking in advance to stay during the non-peak season. Unless you are strongly considering closing your rental, you should keep your calendar open 18 months in advance. We typically hold maximum prices for weekends except for in the slow season for everything 9 months or more out.

Your length-of-stay discount will vary based on your local market and your strategy to capture your specific avatar. This is usually handled in the OTA, not in your pricing software, unfortunately. Some OTA's have different rule sets for businesses than they do for small-time hosts, but we are able to offer length-of-stay discounts automatically in Airbnb. If this feature is not available to you, you can still advertise a length of stay discount in your listing and send a "special offer" to Airbnb. We usually offer a small discount of 3% starting at either three or four nights, depending on the listing and market demand, and scale up to either a 13- to 15% discount for a week. This discount is applied to their entire stay, so it does add up on high-dollar bookings, but you do want to attract stays longer than two nights if you want to have higher occupancy, so it is worth the trade-off. We usually have a 20 percent discount for a month, and we have only landed a couple of those bookings. We don't do the strategy of "book X number of days and get a free night" because there are too many variables to that strategy, and it usually ends up giving too large of a discount. Surprisingly, Vrbo only has an option for weekly and monthly discounts, which I think hurt them. Length of stay discounts are something to look at when building a direct booking website, as ours does not allow for it to be automated, and we have to send guests coupon codes for length of stay.

We get asked fairly regularly about a military or first responder discount, but we do not give discounts for these. As an Army veteran and Iraq

War veteran, I do respect those who serve, but I don't believe offering a discount here is necessary. Fortunately, as a veteran, I can say "as a veteran myself" and not come across as an unpatriotic snob. If you want to give a discount, by all means do so. Just know that many people who ask for a military discount will book even if you politely tell them no.

Some hosts really get into upselling their guests, and this is fine if you do it professionally and have products or services that actually add value to the guests; otherwise, it just feels sleazy and makes them weirded out. As long as you are not too aggressive, you can upsell by offering local gift baskets and products, smore kits and movie night packages, firewood, birthday decorations, or anything of that nature. Airbnb has a whole experience platform where you could even upsell some services to your guests. Just don't make your guests feel like there should be an unsubscribe button in all the messages you are sending them about upsells.

The only upsell that we do across all of our listings is an extra day message that we send out about two weeks from the guest stay, letting them know that the day before or the day after their stay is available if they want to extend their reservation a day at 15% off our normal minimum price. Don't send the message too far out until you are reasonably sure you will not get another booking and your price has already dropped to the minimum price. Unless you have software that does this with automation, just create a template that you can copy and paste to your upcoming guest. It is seasonally successful for us, as guests during more flexible time periods like summer break often extend a day or two, but it is a lot of work, and to date we only have a 2.4% conversion rate on these messages.

To conclude, pricing is something that cannot be overemphasized. It is possibly the easiest way you can shoot yourself in the foot by doing just a couple of things wrong. If you are going to manage your listing yourself, do your research and have a dedicated time each week to review and edit your pricing.

CHAPTER 8

PHOTOS AND LISTING DESCRIPTION

Outside of being listed on all the OTAs and setting up your property correctly, having professional photos and a clear listing description is the most critical component of marketing your property. Your photos and listing description take a relatively small amount of time compared to physically setting up your property, but don't rush through it or try to save a few bucks on professional photos because your setup cost went over budget.

Photos are critical to marketing, and the listing description is critical for educating the potential buyer. Yes, photos have an education component to them, and the listing description has a bit of a marketing component to it, and we will get to that in a moment.

The photos are much more important in selling your space than your description of the space. You can use all the common descriptive terms, like luxurious, spacious, nestled in the woods, and every other phrase that writers feel so proud of and potential guests skim over when looking at the listing. When a potential guest looks for a property, they look at the first few photos and then make a decision if they are going to keep looking.

If they are interested, they will look at the rest of your photos, check your amenities and location, and probably then price and then check your reviews.

Here are some dos and don'ts for photographing your property.

Do:

- Take a picture of the entire surrounding area, including one that shows how your home fits into the surroundings. Aerial photos are very helpful for this. Some people don't take exterior photos, and to me, that screams, "This listing is in a sketchy location; don't book it."
- Take photos at the best time of the year (typically when everything is green and pretty), and have supplemental photos showing snow or the different seasons.
- Have a sufficient, but not excessive, number of Airbnb has a fifty-photo limit, and you should not reach this if you have a small

property. Thirty to forty photos is fine for a small listing.

- Use two or three photos from different angles in the main common spaces.
- Add one or two photos of local attractions. Don't add too many, or that will imply the area is exciting but the home itself is boring.
- Add one or two detail shots of neat decor or detailed features of the house if you have enough photos left.

Do not:

- DIY the photos unless you are actually good or really can't afford to pay a professional and will put the time into doing it right.
- Zoom too far in. Many amateur photos are shot standing halfway in a doorway and only get a fraction of the room, making things seem smaller than they actually are.

I am not a photographer, and whenever we do any photography "in house," one of my more talented team members takes care of them. There are several helpful resources on YouTube specifically for photographing short-term rentals if you decide to take photos yourself, though I would recommend using a professional. Here are a few basic tips from my associates:

- Take photos in landscape orientation.
- Make sure your phone is not tilted so that you have nice, straight lines.
- Stand in the corner of a room to get the best and broadest field of view.
- Use the wide-angle setting on your phone.
- Adjust the brightness of your lighting.
- Don't use filters unless you really know what you are doing, or you may end up with grainy photos.

Preparing for photos is critical for achieving good results; don't just wing it and then try to Photoshop a bunch of random things out of the photos after the fact. Whether or not you take the photos yourself or hire a professional, you will need to be on site before the shoot and make sure things are ready. For example, you will need to make sure to do the following:

Before photo day:

- Make sure you do any occasional maintenance that may reflect in pictures, i.e., pressure washing, gutter or roof cleaning, etc.
- Make sure the landscaping has been done before photos are taken.

- Block off your calendar unless the photographer is very local and flexible.
- Make sure the cleaners are notified and will have it cleaned well before photo time.

Staging notes for the day of photos:

- Make sure covers are off of amenities (grills, pool tables, hot tubs, etc.).
- Make sure outdoor spaces that often get missed, like fire pit areas, are properly staged.
- Make sure after-thought spaces, like the laundry room, are presentable if they are to be photographed.
- Make sure you have the comforters you want on the beds and that the backups are not in use.
- Do not over-stage your property. If you don't normally leave a bottle of wine, put chocolates on the beds, and fold your towels into swans, don't do it for a photo. You want to show potential guests what they can expect to find—no more, no less.

Notes to communicate to the photographer:

- Clarify any part of the property that you want done that the photographer might miss.

PHOTOS AND LISTING DESCRIPTION
PHOTOS AND LISTING DESCRIPTION

- Let them know a bunch of close-ups are not needed, only whole-room photos.
- Because we can only use 50 photos, where possible, take one photo instead of two. For example, if there's a long patio with a hot tub and some furniture, don't take one picture of the hot tub and one of the furniture; go out to the side of the patio and choose an angle where you can get both, with the most important feature closer to the camera.
- Make sure you tell the photographer your maximum file size. The maximum video size for our software is 50 MB.
- Avoid house numbers where possible.
- Avoid signage where possible (house rules, caution signs).
- Make sure to photograph every bathroom (for some reason, this often gets missed).
- Unless it's an impressive walk-in closet, photos of closets are not needed.

Updating your listings with new photos is a lot of work, so if at all possible, get professional photos done right off the bat to reduce the amount of work. Depending on how long it takes the files to load, it takes us about 8 hours of labor to redo the photos for a listing. We have six different OTAs to load, arrange, and label photos on, and sometimes even professional photos take a little work in cropping or editing.

But just because it is a lot of work if you are doing things right and advertising on all major OTAs doesn't give you an excuse to not constantly update and shuffle photos. If you update or add amenities, change significant furniture, or do anything of that nature, update your listing.

When arranging your photos in your listing, you want to choose about five leading images to hook your audience. Airbnb and Vrbo both display five images on the main listing page once a potential guest clicks on your listing. These five images should be your best photos of the most impressive features of your house, preferably major amenities, a nice shot or two of the common areas, and at least one exterior photo of the home.

After these photos, your photo order should be in line with how a guest would likely tour your home, and each photo should be labeled clearly. If you had common areas and a master on the main, you would label each photo as such. For example, "living area on main floor," "kitchen on main floor," and "master bedroom with King bed on main floor". Then move on to another floor and label those rooms specifically as well, so the guest is following along with you. Make sure you describe what size bed is in each bedroom photo and label any sleeper sofa accordingly. You will get a lot of questions from potential guests about sleeping arrangements, and this will reduce your customer service.

We also create a floor plan for each of our listings and include it as an image in the listing. If the home has more than one floor, there is one image per floor. Since we began doing this, we have had a large reduction in the questions we receive about how the home is laid out. This is especially important in larger homes, where often multiple couples or families are sharing the space, and they want to know before booking how they will utilize the space and have privacy. We used a paid software platform, floorplanner.com, for our listings and have found them to be reasonably priced for the software they provide.

Two other options related to photos that are worth considering are a video tour and a 3D or 360-degree virtual tour. Airbnb does not allow for video, but we are able to include a YouTube link to our video tours in our Vrbo listings. Many photographers now offer either a video tour or a 360-degree virtual tour with their photography, and I think adding at least one is a good way to stand out from your competition. Video tours are more effective for larger groups, again because of the increase in planning for how they will utilize and share the space. A video tour is created by stringing together photos, but you can film your own live video on your phone and upload it to YouTube if you do not hire a professional. The more ways you can give potential guests a live snapshot of your property, the better. Occasionally, potential guests ask if they can stop by and look at a property before booking, and it's good to have a video you can point them to if you can't accommodate a tour.

Let's begin the discussion of the listing description with the title. A unique listing title does catch the eye, but don't panic if you can't think of one. The listing title should convey the overall feel of the property, so choose an appropriate noun that best fits your space, whether that be a lodge, cottage, or bungalow. List your top amenities in your headline, as most travelers won't fill out the search filters when skimming through properties, and even if they weren't specifically looking for one with a hot tub, seeing that amenity in your listing could earn a click. Typically, you don't want to waste characters on the number of bedrooms or occupancy of the space, as these are obvious to the guests and probably in their search filter.

One trick that we use is to put "New Listing" in the title until we get ten reviews. This lets guests know why we don't have many or any reviews. On non-Airbnb channels, it may take a while to get ten reviews, as other OTAs don't push travelers to leave reviews like Airbnb does.

Writing the actual listing description can be a bit trickier to nail than you would think. These days, many people fancy themselves as writers but are not, just like many people fancy themselves as photographers but are not. I want to clarify right off the bat that travelers won't book because of fluffy copy. It is good to introduce the guests to your space and describe how they can enjoy it, but you will still want to keep it brief. This is because guests do not like to read the listing. Half of our customer service issues are from people not reading the listing, and we have very clear and organized listing descriptions. I really want to put a note at the top of each listing that says PLEASE READ LISTING IN ITS ENTIRETY BEFORE

BOOKING, but I feel that could come across as a bit aggressive.

Typically, we try to walk our guests through the space, just hitting the highlights on each floor. Make sure you explain in your copy and in your photo tags what size beds you have.

It is okay to sell, but don't oversell and don't be long-winded, or the important notes and disclosures of your listing will get lost in the weeds and you will have complaints. The tone of your writing should be casual but professional, just like your customer service responses.

I have seen many clever hosts display a lot of the information in bullet-style format. I think this is excellent and can make the information easy to process. Long paragraphs lose guest attention. We use an FAQ section at the bottom of the listing to educate guests, and this is where we disclose pet fees, early check-in fees, etc. I have also seen the use of emojis becoming more prevalent in listing descriptions, and I believe it does make the listing seem a little more friendly but also a little unprofessional if used frequently.

You do not want to add anything that most people won't care about, such as your family's history with the property, unless it is legitimately a historic property or it is something very unique, like a five-generation family farm. Most people only care about themselves and are interested in learning how they can have an enjoyable trip, not the history of your property. Even some practical details, like having high thread count sheets or luxury towels, are really good bonuses to be discovered by the guest on site and will most likely not cause your guest to choose your property over someone else's', and therefore should be left out of the listing description to keep it from getting too long.

Somewhere in your listing description, you absolutely must disclose any property quirks or potential issues for guests. It is far, far better to not get a booking than to trick someone into booking when they would not have given all the information. Not disclosing a bad access road, a shared space, or an amenity will get you slammed in a review and in your accuracy rating on Airbnb. It is fine to put a positive spin on a slight issue, as long as you aren't underselling the issue. If your driveway is horrific and requires a high-clearance vehicle with 4WD, don't try to pass it off as a couple of fun bumps in the road.

PHOTOS AND LISTING DESCRIPTION

I would recommend writing out your listing description, disclosures, and house rules, and then getting someone else who also knows your property, such as a spouse or business partner, to also write the listing copy independently from you. When you are both done, compare notes and create a blended copy. It is also a good practice to spend some time looking at your competitors listings, as you will find a few things that you forgot to highlight, such as a popular venue or attraction nearby that you should mention in your listing or add to your guidebook. See what they advertise and how they advertise, but don't copy it.

As soon as you publish your listing, have someone with fresh eyes check it for grammatical errors and any information that may be incomplete or unclear to the consumer. Congratulations! The race has just begun. Just because your listing is published doesn't mean that you should not update it. You should be updating it several times in the first 30 days as you get questions from potential guests and feedback from your first few guests on what they loved about the property but didn't realize prior to booking and what they didn't like about it that you may need to disclose. Avoid the temptation to edit your listing based on one person's feedback, but if

you get the same question multiple times, don't be
stubborn about giving it a tune-up.

CHAPTER 9

PHYSICAL PRODUCTS

A lot of actually stitching a tougher net comes down to the physical products you put in your home. Some of them are expensive and will only be changed every 5–15 years if you choose wisely. Some are consumables and will be part of your revolving expenditures, which you need to nail to meet and exceed guest expectations without eating too deep into your bottom line. Some may find this chapter boring, but for someone who loves the operations part of the business, this is where I find strange satisfaction in trying to find out how to save $7 a year on hand soap without compromising quality.

We are going to drop items into the following categories: furniture, outdoor furniture and large items, appliances, game amenities, technology, household goods, decor, linens, supplies, and cleaning supplies.

We are going to start with bigger items, as you should when setting up a house, and work our way to the cheaper consumables. Estimating the entire cost of a setup is a difficult task, but the things that move the needle the most are obviously the big-ticket items: furniture and appliances. Get these right and on budget first, and you should have enough jingle in your pocket to also buy the cutesy stuff you saw on Pinterest. I highly recommend setting a budget and setting an estimated expense for each item on a spreadsheet before you begin. If you splurge on one area, you must find a way to make up for it somewhere else. There is a fine line between being a cheapskate and being too loose in your spending, and you must contemplate each decision before pulling the trigger. You don't want to be like the guy in the action movie who is fighting off a 100-person assault force with three magazines of ammo and just sprays bullets all over the place and runs out of ammo way too soon. There is no hero coming to save you when you run out of ammo; you need to conserve your ammo and take the shots that count. However, you don't want to be the penny pincher that furnishes an expensive home with cheap products and supplies and constantly has to replace items on top of getting critical reviews.

The last note on the overall cost of your setup is time. Yes, time is a cost, and a costly cost. Whether or not you have a mortgage payment, you have time-associated costs like taxes, insurance, utilities, etc. So while you may not want to hire help to set up your home and want to do it on the weekends or on a few trips to your property to "save money," do that math before making that decision. I understand that some people really enjoy decorating and setting up a home, and there is nothing wrong with that. But I highly recommend hiring someone to speed you up, whether that be doing the punch list on the home, such as painting or landscaping, or assembling furniture for you. Find someone to do what you are not great at to speed you up. I have seen furnishing a short-term rental take 60 days longer than necessary, add thousands in direct overhead, and lose thousands in opportunity costs. Sometimes, when setting up properties that I own or lease, I have had to bite the bullet and pay for rustic end tables and coffee tables that I wanted to build myself and pay people to do things that I am perfectly capable of doing myself. Time can get unfriendly to your bottom line in a hurry, so just make sure you are operating off of a calculator and not your preferences.

Furniture: Furniture should be ordered as soon as possible, but not rushed.

Make sure you have measured your spaces and know what size couch, beds, etc. will fit. If you do not live near the property, I recommend creating a floor plan of your home to include door and window locations so that you can order furniture remotely. I would also recommend not starting to bring stuff into a home that is undergoing painting, flooring, or any other significant update. I can't tell you the number of times that I have seen furniture and household goods being moved around and getting dirty or damaged when they showed up before the work was done. If you have to have items delivered, store them away from the action and in a clean environment as much as possible.

Beds: We recommend king beds whenever possible, but if you can't fit a king bed, just get the largest bed your space can accommodate. Avoid the temptation to save $150 on a smaller bedding option or use a full bed instead of a queen because that's what you already have. Most couples would prefer a larger bed, and some will exclusively book places that have a king bed. I don't think full beds are a good option anymore, unless it is a daybed or overflow sleeping area. Not even newlyweds want to share a full bed and catch an elbow in the face.

King bed frames can be problematic, as most do not have a very good center support leg, and they often break in the middle. I would not buy any bed with Allen key bolts. Short-term rentals need to be designed for commercial use. If you buy a cheap king-size bed, come up with a way to reinforce the middle of it, or expect it to break. We build our own beds out of dimensional lumber so that they are unbreakable, and we give them solid bases on all sides so cleaners can't miss underwear or another embarrassing item lost under the bed. I have had many beds break during my management, but most of them are the Ikea style with threaded bolts and thin gauge metal that fails with enough use or with a certain amount of body weight and bed movement. Non-industrial metal bunk beds will squeak and creak and, over time, will sag and fall apart. You can only tighten up those little aluminum keys so many times before they strip, so you want to stick with commercial bunks with welded joints or old-fashioned wood bunk beds.

We send out surveys to all of our guests after their stay, and by far the second favorite choice after a king bed is a queen bed with a trundle underneath. A little bit of this depends on your target clientele, if you are going for couples retreats or more geared towards groups where people want separate sleeping options and don't want to be in the same bed as someone else (i.e., bachelor parties, cyclist groups, motorcycle trips). You want to create as many different sleeping options as possible to accommodate different types of groups, and trundles are a great alternative to bunk beds. Many insurance companies are getting picky about bunk beds due to liability, and cleaners hate making bunk beds. Kids will play on the top bunk and wreck it, forcing the cleaners to wash the linens and remake the bed nearly every time, even if it is not used. Trundles are much quicker and safer than bunk beds. If you do decide to go with a bunk bed, make sure you have good head clearance to the ceiling, a good distance to the nearest ceiling fan, or anything like that. Try not to have the bunk bed against the window if possible, as that always creates issues with kids pulling on curtains or blinds. Having a twin-over-full or twin-over-queen-size bunk is a better option than a standard twin-over-twin bunk, especially if they are tall enough and have room for an adult to sit up in the bottom bunk. If you can get an outlet, light, or bin for the guest staying in the top bunk to put their phone or other items in, that is a nice touch that guests appreciate.

You really need to have legitimate sleeping options for the maximum occupancy you allow in your listing. Saying you sleep 10 but having one queen bed and four queen air mattresses will not lead to good reviews or reviews. If you don't have

"real beds" for all your guests, these are our preferred alternative options in order of preference:

- Trundle beds
- Sleeper sofas
- Roll out cots
- Air mattresses

I'm going to stray from conventional wisdom now and say I don't think it is worth spending extra money on high-end mattresses. Whenever we do a setup, we buy mattresses from Amazon for a few hundred bucks and get great feedback from guests. You can drop $800 or $1400 per mattress, but it doesn't seem to move the needle in guest satisfaction, and I think you should put that savings towards upgrading something that is a little more visible.

We do recommend spending a little extra and getting a mattress encasement and a slip-on mattress protector for each mattress. Many guests will change the sheets during their stay or will strip the bed and start laundry for you, so what is underneath needs to look presentable. Mattress encasements are necessary for bed bug proofing as well as stopping anything that leaks through the first line of defense. So why do you need the slip-on mattress cover as well? Because zippered mattress encasements are more expensive, generally take two people to put back on, and are a nightmare to wash, It's like trying to wash a giant zip-lock bag, and there are just pockets of water everywhere, and you can't get in the dryer with any heat. Don't make your cleaner deal with that; just buy a mattress protector to put on top of your encasement.

Pillows: In the master bedroom, we will do a couple of king-size pillows and some decorative pillows, but for the most part, we just buy the standard-size pillow from Walmart. We put at least two pillows out for each bed (full size and up), with a couple extra in each closet. Some people like flat pillows, some like fluffy pillows, so we try to keep a variety on site. We do recommend using zippered pillow encasements, though they get really expensive for king-size pillows.

Dressers: Don't overspend here. Most people don't unpack. If the room is small, it's ok to put a chest of drawers in the closet or even go without one in a non-primary bedroom, so long as you have some hooks and a couple of nightstands with drawers.

Couches: Take your time selecting couches. Couches are not easy to get or get rid of, and they are not something you want to be changing or upgrading every year or two. If you have a matching set, a very specific arrangement for a sectional you need, or a sleeper sofa, they are even more difficult to replace.

Generally, you want to use real leather. You can typically find a nice used leather couch for about 30% of what they cost new and still get five or more years out of them, depending on where they are located in the home and what kind of occupancy you do. We condition our leather couches about twice a year. Some types of faux leather are okay in certain situations, but they typically do not hold up to pets or abuse very well. If one of your couch cushions gets damaged, sometimes you can get by with a cushion cover for a couple of years.

One thing you don't want to do is get a reclining sofa, and especially not a power reclining sofa. As a general rule for furniture, you don't want any moving parts unless they are absolutely necessary. Guests are rough with things, don't know how to use buttons and controls, and constantly unplug everything. Recliners and reclining sofas also make more hiding spots for things to fall into that cleaners can miss, so you're better off to just stick to the basics.

Chairs and Stools: We have fairly consistent issues with chairs and bar stools breaking. If you have a large dining room table, I would highly recommend benches with just two sturdy chairs at each end of the table. Most dining room chairs are not designed for commercial use, and anything with a threaded connection will wiggle loose and break. Swivel bar stools are obviously a bad idea. We have some units with bar stools that have only welded joints, and they give us zero problems. Any cushions on bar stools or kitchen chairs are also a pretty bad idea, as they will get stained and tired looking pretty quickly.

Outdoor furniture and large items: Outdoor furniture is very dependent on the expectations of your market. While urban markets may require little to no outdoor furniture, markets where the outdoors are a large part of the draw require usable outdoor spaces for guests to enjoy the experience. Outdoor furniture is easy to miss and often overlooked by cleaners and staff, so make sure that someone is checking the quality and cleanliness of outdoor furniture.

As much as possible, don't use real wood unless it is under a covered porch. It just does not hold up to the sun and weather. Those wood Adirondack chairs look so nice in photos, but you will replace them or restain them so quickly. We have had a bad experience with foldable and adjustable Adirondack chairs that confuse guests who just try to force them and end up breaking them. The more moving parts, the more things will break.

Swings are a nice touch, but if they are large enough to hold two people, four people will get on there and goof around and break it. I have had guests break two porch swings by ripping the lags out of the support beams, both of which passed the test of my trying to break them prior to the first guest. I would recommend a warning sign and commercial porch swing hangers if you are going to use one.

Fire pits are expected in our market, and they do add value to the guest experience. Fire pit seating can be a bit tricky; wood stumps will get torn up and destroyed pretty quickly. Adirondack chairs are a decent option but are fairly expensive for the thick plastic versions. In some of our units, we have benches built out of pressure-treated lumber with 6x6's in the ground, which is the most durable option we have come up with so far. Gas fire pits are a good alternative if you have a covered porch. Just be aware that you will have lots of propane tanks to exchange unless you can get a gas line directly to the firepit.

If at all possible, create an outdoor eating space large enough to accommodate the entire group you are hosting. If the weather is nice, that is where guests want to eat.

Picnic tables are probably the best casual option overall, as they are nearly indestructible and you have the seating built in. A coat of stain on the picnic table will class it up a little bit. A nicer glass top or metal outdoor table with cushion seats is great for a higher-end rental, but the cushions are a lot of work for the cleaners and will have to be replaced fairly regularly. Don't expect the guests to put cushions in the outdoor storage bin to keep them out of the rain and sun when not in use. If you have an outdoor umbrella over your outdoor table, make sure it is properly anchored, and try to get the guests (or cleaners) to put the umbrella down when not in use. When they are left open, they are a giant sail, and I have had them blow away in wind storms and cause damage.

Grills: Having a grill is a standard feature in our market. Make sure your cleaner does not forget to clean it. We ask guests to clean it after use, but they rarely do. Propane grills are preferred by more guests, but there are a large enough number of charcoal users that you may be able to get away with a charcoal-only grill. Many guests can't light a propane grill and think the propane tank is empty when it is not. You want to keep at least one spare propane tank on site, and make sure you are testing any tanks that guests say are empty. Because of the aggravation and expense of propane tanks, we are trying to switch over to charcoal and have the guests provide their own charcoal. You really can't expect a guest to go out and purchase a propane tank to grill out, but we don't get pushback for not providing charcoal.

Hot Tub:

Hot tubs are a huge draw in our market and are also a huge amount of work. If you are not considering a hot tub, you can skip this section.

There is a little bit of a learning curve, both for you as the owner of the hot tub and for the cleaner. Having a hot tub and being pet friendly is kind of our niche in our market, as both are fairly rare, and 76% of our units have a hot tub and 96% of our units are pet friendly. I will briefly describe some dos and don'ts on purchasing and setting up a hot tub, and then some cleaning and maintenance tips that you should know whether or not you are the one actually cleaning the hot tub. Many cleaners get intimidated by hot tubs and will require coaching to successfully sanitize a hot tub. Small homes or cabins that appeal to couples on getaways benefit the most from hot tubs. They are also helpful on larger units, especially in our slow season of January through March, but their biggest impact is on small to mid-size homes.

The first thing to consider when purchasing a hot tub is whether you have a good location for it and can get it to that location. You need a level pad roughly 8 feet by 8 feet, preferably with a walking area on at least three sides so your cleaners can reach the inside of the tub. A gravel pad is okay, a concrete pad is best, and a deck should not be used unless it is properly and professionally reinforced. Most hot tubs have 300–400 gallons of water, so you're looking at about 4,000 lb of dead weight before the six people get in. Risking this on a deck that is not designed for it is not a risk you want to take. An empty hot tub is not all that heavy, but it is awkward and often difficult to get where you want it to go. I have lifted one with one other person using appliance carry straps, but my back was not right for a couple months after. Most big-box retailers will deliver it for free to your driveway but will not carry it down to your pad or take it up on your deck. Make sure your pad is fairly level, as just a couple of inches of slope will cause the water to be way too high on one side if it's barely covering the jets on the other side. If possible, choose a covered location or build a roof over the hot tub. This will allow your guests to use the hot tub no matter what the weather, as well as keep leaves and debris out of the hot tub and extend the lifespan of your hot tub cover. If you are able to have a roof over your hot tub, hang some string lights to finish creating a nice ambiance for your guests.

The next component to consider is the electrical. I would not recommend a plug-and-play hot tub, as they cannot maintain temperature in cold environments and take too long to heat up on the same day. A 240-volt circuit from your breaker panel is pretty expensive, so make sure you get a quote from an electrician before deciding to purchase. In our market, it usually costs about $1,500–$2,500 to get a power run to the hot tub. Make sure that your home has the capacity to add another 240-volt circuit to it, as many homes are at the maximum number of breaker slots as well as close to the maximum capacity of amperage for their home. Many large homes still have only a 200-amp service, so if your hot tub installation requires you to upgrade your meter base and panel, it will most likely not be worth the expense.

You also need to figure out the orientation of your hot tub before installation. Normally the wiring comes into the base of the hot tub on the side with a display, but check prior to purchase so you don't have the electrical conduit on the surface where it could be a tripping hazard. It's not ideal for your guests to be climbing into the hot tub over the display, and you definitely do not want them climbing over the filter housing.

PHYSICAL PRODUCTS

Make sure you have a good set of hot tub stairs. This is not somewhere where I would try to save a few dollars by building my own set of stairs due to liability. You can get a set of plastic stairs online for about $75. If your concrete pad has a smooth finish on it, you should put a sealer down with some grit in it to keep people from slipping, or at least put an outdoor mat at the foot of the stairs to keep guests from slipping as they step down from the last step. Make sure you have a Slippery When Wet sign up near the hot tub as well as a hot tub rules sign.

Make sure that whatever location you have has easy water access, as your cleaners will need to frequently change the water. If possible, a hot water source is an ideal situation for same-day turns. Even with a 240-volt hot tub with a 4-KW heater in it, it will only heat up about 4° per hour, so if your cleaners have to dump the entire hot tub, it will be cold when the next guest checks in on the same day. Some manufacturers say you are not supposed to fill a hot tub with hot water, but we have not had an issue with this at the homes where we do this. The ideal situation is to have two hose bibs near the hot tub, one with hot water and one with cold water, so that you can use both at the same time and refill the tub in about 30 minutes, but this is usually not possible except for when specifically planned for in a newly constructed home.

You will want to set up your hot tub with a gravity drain. Most manufacturers have them built into the hot tub, but they are all a little bit different. Your cleaner should be able to just turn the shut-off valve and drain the hot tub without having to siphon or pump it. We typically drain the hot tub into a gutter drain or bury a section of hose so that it does not erode the immediate area with weekly draining. If you do not have enough water for weekly draining or if your water bill is super expensive, I would not consider getting a hot tub.

The last thing you need to consider is whether or not you will have a cover lift. If you do not have any type of cover lift or shelf for your guests to slide the cover on, the cover will end up wherever the guest decides to throw it. New hot tub covers are very expensive and are a pain to clean, so when guests don't have a good spot to put them and there's not a cover lift, it will shorten the lifespan of your hot tub cover. A new hot tub cover for a full-size hot tub starts at about $600, so it's not something that you want to replace frequently.

Cover lifts take a little bit of knowledge and skill to install, so that is something I would have professionally installed if that were an option. Another style of hot tub lift is a simple shelf on one side of the hot tub. The user can flip the hot tub cover in half and then just slide it onto the shelf so it is out of their way. These are pretty simple and straightforward and don't have a lot of issues as there's no moving parts.

Now let's take a look at maintaining a hot tub. We use a chlorine-based system, as we have found a bromine-based system is more expensive and not potent enough to keep up with guests constant use. We use chlorine granules instead of floats for faster dispersion of the chlorine. Be sure you refer to professional guidelines and your manufacturer's recommendation for your volume of water, but it only takes a pinch of chlorine a week to maintain chlorine in a hot tub and about a third of a cup if you have to dump and refill it. Since we use a chlorine-based system, we use a non-chlorine-based shock to help break down organics in the water and clean up the water to try to avoid dumping it all the time. We also use a defoamer to knock down those bubbles that should not be there and a clarifier to help deal with any water clarity issues. Do not put too much effort into saving the water unless you have to; sometimes there is no substitute for just dumping the water and starting over.

Power should be turned off to the hot tub before you ever start draining it; if the power is left on when draining, you can damage your hot tub. I would recommend keeping a pump on hand to remove the water faster on same-day turns. I would also highly recommend a hot tub vacuum to siphon out dirt and debris that settle at the bottom of the hot tub. These little vacuums will also help with the gravity drain, but do not drain the hot tub quickly. The hot tub filter should be rinsed out after every guest and swapped out with a clean filter every time the hot tub is super gross. If the water is gross, that means the filter is gross. We have a system for collecting hot tub filters at the homes we manage and bringing them back to our shop to sanitize, dry, and then return them to the homes. What system you choose to implement will largely depend on the price of the hot tub filters, as they can range from as cheap as $15 to as high as $60. Always keep the hot tub cover on when you're not actively cleaning the tub, as having the cover off will let bugs and debris in the hot tub and let heat escape. This is also a common issue with guests complaining about the hot tub not being hot while they leave the cover off while not in use.

When deciding which hot tub to purchase, no matter what, you want to avoid bells and whistles. This is more important in your hot tub than in anything else. Guests will get in a hot tub and just start pushing buttons on the display, so they often end up putting the hot tub into sleep or economy mode, which means it will never reach temperature. Many guests book a property because of the hot tub, so any issue with the hot tub causes a lot of problems with the guests. It doesn't really matter if it's the guests fault or the hot tub's fault; if they put it in the wrong mode and it's not functional, they will complain about it and give you a bad review or request a refund. Hot tubs are most commonly used at night, which means the message regarding any issues with the hot tub will also be at night. If your hot tub does have different modes, you need instructions on site on how to reset it if this happens and a warning on your hot tub sign about what the display should and should not read. Most hot tubs will show if they are in economy mode or sleep mode and will only display the temperature if they are in standard mode.

Well, those are the very basics for hot tubs, but don't let all those steps or issues scare you. If you have a small cabin, this is probably the best move you can make that will differentiate you from other listings.

APPLIANCES

Having reliable appliances is important because when something goes down, it can cause quite a scramble for whoever is in charge of operations. If your washer or dryer goes down and your cleaner is using them on site, they better have extra linens on hand or a plan to get them done quickly for a turn. If the HVAC or fridge stops working, be prepared to refund guests and pay an emergency repair bill. Most big-box stores like Home Depot do not carry appliances you can pick up that day anymore. You have to place an order and wait a week or two for delivery, especially if you want a choice of appliance color or brand. Often, repairing appliances costs more than they are worth, so you need to build out some options in case of emergencies.

PHYSICAL PRODUCTS

Finding reliable and relatively inexpensive appliance technicians is difficult, but at least it is in our market. It can cost $150 just to have your appliance diagnosed and find out it isn't worth replacing. Having a used appliance dealer is a helpful option. We have one vendor who we love who will show up with a used washing machine, bring parts he thinks may be the issue with our current washer, but if it's not, sell us the used washer and haul off the old one for the parts. This is the ideal situation because he doesn't charge a trip charge or diagnosis fee if he sells us the used washer. When troubleshooting an appliance, use this thing called Google, and after doing so, try to get an appliance guy to give you a couple of other things to check over the phone when you call to schedule the appointment.

Because of all the difficulties with appliances, I highly recommend getting simple, quality appliances without any upgraded options.

Washer and Dryers: If possible, provide a washer and dryer and laundry detergent for guests. We label our washing machines, asking guests not to put in more than six towels at a time, because overloading a washing machine is the best way to shorten its lifespan.

Front-load washers use less water and have faster cycle times, and without the agitator in the middle, they can wash a larger comforter, but again, be careful not to overload. A good washer and dryer set will keep your cleaners happy, especially on a same-day turn, so they don't have to take laundry offsite. When laundry goes off-site, sometimes it doesn't all come back. Do some research on your washer if you are buying a new one. Many washers now have a twenty-minute quick-wash cycle, which is very helpful.

Dryers have significantly fewer issues than washers, and most of their issues revolve around the duct. Make sure your cleaning crew is cleaning out the lint filter every time, and your maintenance crew is checking and cleaning the duct lines as needed. We have an anemometer we use on maintenance checks to make sure the airflow is where it is supposed to be.

Ovens and Ranges: Ovens don't typically give us a lot of trouble, but we would recommend putting tin foil at the bottom of the oven to catch a lot of the crumbs and grease. We do provide an oven cleaner and degreaser at every unit, making it easy for our cleaners and guests to maintain them, as we do occasionally get complaints about the racks or bottoms of the oven not being clean. Although gas ranges are typically considered higher-end, we prefer electric glass top ranges for their cleanability. Also, some guests get really scared of gas, so if anything is wrong with a burner, they could consider it a safety issue. We have had one of our listings temporarily suspended on Airbnb for a guest being worried about a gas burner, even though it was a non-issue.

Microwave: Most of our microwaves are over the range, and they typically don't give us trouble until they randomly die. When they break, 98% of the time, they are not worth repairing. Make the microwave a priority item for cleaning inspections, as cleaners often forget to wipe down the microwave.

Refrigerator and Freezer: The most common trouble we have with refrigerators and freezers has to do with the ice maker. Whether it quits working all together or the ice gets stuck on a guest and they try to force things, it is a pretty common problem. They are also very expensive to fix, so if yours goes out, consider getting a freestanding countertop ice maker. Make sure your cleaner has a good system for wiping down the fridge and freezer and knows what to leave and what to throw away. They should not be leaving any condiments behind that were used by previous guests.

Dishwasher: A fast cycle is also helpful on a dishwasher. Many of the newer and nicer dishwashers have a minimum run time of a couple of hours. Make sure someone is routinely inspecting and wiping down the gaskets and inside of the dishwasher and cleaning up any gunk or buildup.

Fireplaces: If you have an indoor fireplace, the fuel type matters. People struggle lighting gas fireplaces, no matter how clear the instructions you provide. I would not do a gas fireplace if I was self-managing and had to take calls late at night to help a guest follow the lighting instructions. If you are hiring a management company, that's their problem, unless, of course, they don't do a good job of responding to guests and you get bad reviews for it. We make sure the gas pilot is on during our weekly walkthroughs because we are so tired of service calls for gas fireplaces.

Guests seem to love wood-burning fireplaces, but they are messy. If you have a wood-burning fireplace, make sure the guest opens the fireplace before use. Electric fireplaces are probably the simplest and lowest risk, but they also are not as much of an attraction for guests and don't help during a power outage.

Ceiling Fans: If you install or replace a ceiling fan, do not, under any circumstances, install one with a remote. Remotes are a nightmare in general, and fan remotes add no value and a whole lot of complications. Remotes go missing, the batteries are custom and die without notice, and guests can't figure out how to use them, so the fan just stays on. Also, make sure your ceiling fan, and all your light fixtures, for that matter, have the standard E26 or A19 base and not a custom bulb that you have to do research and place a special order for. Also, never buy a fixture that has no changeable bulb. Yes, that cool LED fixture may last a long time, but maybe it won't, and you want something that your cleaner can swap a light bulb in, not something you have to order a new fixture and schedule a handyman to install.

HVAC: Your heating and air conditioning are massive expenses and are by far the most expensive and important appliances in your home. At a minimum, you need someone regularly changing the filters, and preferably someone who is able to swap out a condensate pump or clear a drain line. We typically use Merv 8 or Merv 11 filters; anything too fine and they will get dirty too quickly and restrict air flow. You can also extend the life of your filters and keep your unit clean by not letting the fan run unnecessarily. Every guest in the world likes to just hit the buttons on the thermostat and turn the fan on instead of auto, so make sure you are checking that when on site and on your thermostat app if you have control there.

The heating and air system is one of the hardest calls to make on expensive repairs vs. replacement, so you certainly want to extend the life of your unit as long as possible. A lack of heat or air conditioning is one of the most common reasons for complaints and customer refunds, so if a unit goes down, you have a big expense coming from both directions.

Mini splits and ductless systems: I used to love mini splits, and I still tolerate them because they are so efficient, but now I believe that the cons outweigh the pros. Typically, the remotes are way too complicated for guests, and the indoor portion

is a pain to clean and maintain. Some remodeling situations make it almost impossible to go with a traditional ducted system, but now that they have variable-speed compressors in traditional systems,

I believe a traditional ducted system is the way to go whenever possible.

Because each mini split head has its own remote, but the entire system can only do either AC or heat, guests often throw the system into error by having one unit in heat and one in AC. You can put it in the information binder, but it won't help; you will still have to be on the phone with the guest, guiding them on how to reset the breaker and explaining how the system works.

Water Heater: Tankless water heaters are a great addition to a rental if you have to replace one or have the chance to upgrade. As they become more common, people who live in large homes who have one are likely to complain about having to stagger showers or running out of hot water. They are very expensive to replace. Try to avoid a condensation pump and have a gravity drain if at all possible. Gas tank less heaters have very few issues, and electric tankless heaters have a lot of issues, in my experience.

Game Amenities:

Having a game room is a huge bonus, especially for larger groups. We don't label our properties as having a "game room" unless it is a dedicated space that has at least two major games. If the home has a garage, we typically utilize it as a game room, as you don't typically derive much value from having a place for guests to park but do from having a dedicated game space. If you use a garage, most likely it will not have heating and cooling, and so you may have to use a space heater in the winter and a window unit or portable AC unit in the summer, or invest in a ductless system.

These are the five core game amenities in our area, and their ranking as the number one choice by guests in our surveys:

Pool Table: 27%

Ping Pong: 23%

Air Hockey: 20%

Foosball: 16%

Poker Table: 14%

Most amenities have a few hiccups and annoying parts to them, so I will go over them briefly.

Pool Table: Make sure you have plenty of space so that your guests can walk around the table in all directions and are not hitting the wall with their pool sticks. Get a short pool stick, also known as a "shorty," if you are tight to one wall. Make sure there are no windows near the table, or someone will find it with their pool stick.

Pool sticks do occasionally break, and pool cue tips do need to be replaced. Make sure your floor is relatively level for a pool table if it's in a garage, as many garages have a pitch to the concrete; if it's not too far off, you can make it up with some shims or small blocks of wood. You can usually find a used table for a decent price, as many people inherit them or end up reselling them when they don't get used, but moving a pool table is very difficult. If you have to disassemble and reassemble a table, factor that into your costs. Cleaning and maintaining the felt is a little bit of work, but usually not that big of a deal. Get a pool table with simple net pockets, not the kind with a ball return, as the balls will get stuck internally, which is a nightmare to resolve without taking apart the table.

Ping Pong: Make sure you calculate for players stepping back to return a serve when calculating space. They do make different sizes of tables, and it's better to have an appropriate size table for the space than to jam in a full-size table and have no room to play.

It's a good idea to label your table with a note that says "No sitting or leaning," as we have had multiple broken ping pong tables. A commercial-grade table is worth the money if you can afford it. Nets always seem to be trouble, so keep a spare net on hand, as well as plenty of spare balls and a couple of extra paddles, as they get beat up and broken fairly often.

Air Hockey: Make sure you have a power supply nearby and have extra pushers and pucks available. Even more expensive pushers tend to get cracked and broken, but they still last longer than the super-cheap ones. If the pucks are too lightweight and cheap, they will go flying off the table and be unplayable. I would not install an air hockey table within range of a window. Electronic scorekeepers often malfunction and break, so expect to have to pivot to an old-fashioned manual score counter. As with all amenities, err on the more commercial side, even if that means you have to buy used. If you buy used, turn the table on and check for dead spots in the table before purchasing.

Foosball: Foosball tables take forever to assemble, so factor that in if you decide to buy a new one. You are better off buying a used commercial-grade table than a cheap new one. Keep extra balls on site, as they will go missing.

Poker Table: A poker table has the fewest issues as there are no moving parts, but it also has the least perceived value from guests and takes up a considerable amount of space. The most aggravating part is maintaining the felt, as guests often eat at the poker table. If you provide a poker table, provide poker chips and some cards. Don't waste your time checking to see if the cards are there. I'm sure none of our decks are full, but we don't get complaints about that.

A few other games you might consider are a shuffleboard table, darts, an indoor basketball hoop game, and a video game console.

A shuffleboard table takes up a lot of space and is expensive. Shuffleboard powder is also messy and can create an almost invisible residue when it inevitably gets all over the floor, which the cleaners can miss but guests can feel with their bare feet.

Darts are still very popular, but check with your insurance before setting one up.

Know that guests will not be accurate and will put holes in everything in the area. Darts also have a short lifespan, so buy them in bulk and keep extras on hand.

An arcade-style indoor basketball hoop is a nice touch; just keep a ball pump on hand. A cabinet-style arcade machine is a good choice for video games, as long as it is user-friendly and has a good variety of games. If you don't make a good purchase, these can be too expensive for the value provided. Other video game systems where guests would have to bring their own games or guests could take, break, or lose remotes or games will have significant costs, questions from guests, and issues.

Overall, a game room is usually a solid investment, and there is typically not a lot of additional annual cost if you buy quality products. You may need to stay on top of cleaners, as I have seen game rooms not get the attention that the rest of the house gets. If you are on the fence about which games to offer, measure out your space carefully and do your market research as to what your competition is providing and if you should try to match their offering or pivot into something a little different.

TECHNOLOGY

Wi-Fi thermostats: Wi-Fi thermostats are a technology that is a no-brainer. We use the Honeywell thermostats, as they seem to be the most user-friendly and have the simplest app. Just know that if you get a thermostat setup and are monitoring it on your phone, people are weird in their selections of temperatures, and it will drive you crazy to see what is going on. What is a comfortable temperature for most guests? 75 in the winter and 65 in the summer. Why? I don't know; I guess they figure they are paying good money, so they might as well run up your power bill. I don't know why most apps don't have governors to restrict how low or high you can turn the temperature, but they don't.

Having control of your thermostat and being able to turn it down and up in between guests will not only save you money on your power bill but will also extend the lifespan of your unit. Wi-Fi thermostats are also handy in giving you a heads up if your system is not heating or cooling properly and when your internet may be out, which are two of our biggest causes for refunds. We have had multiple instances where the thermostat app gave us a heads-up on a Wi-Fi or HVAC issue that we were able to resolve before the guest checked in and we had to refund them.

If guests are out of control with the thermostat, be careful how you proceed with making an adjustment. It is pretty common for guests who are hot to turn on the AC as low as it will go, as if the AC will magically work faster if it is set to a low number. So if I see something crazy, I just check back a little while later. I do occasionally make adjustments, usually at about 5:00 in the morning when I'm awake, but assume the guest is not. If they have the AC set to 65, I will bump it up to 69 and hope that they will assume someone else in their group did it at some point in the night. So far, I haven't been questioned by the guest.

The Wi-Fi thermostat is a huge advantage after guests check out, as most cleaners forget to make an adjustment or may not be on site right away. If a guest checks out on a Monday and the next checks in on a Friday, that is a long period to be heating or cooling a space, so I adjust thermostats right after guests check out and the morning before they arrive.

TV's and Projectors: Some of our homes have a TV in every bedroom, as well as all the major common areas, and I think this is best practice if possible. The price of smart TVs has come way down, and at a minimum, you should have a large TV in the living area (at least 55") and a decent-sized TV in the master bedroom. Because of the room arrangement and location of doors and closets, it's not always possible to get a TV wall mounted opposite the bed in every bedroom, but that is ideal if the setup allows for it and if you can afford it. Wall mounting is preferred to TV stands, as it has a cleaner look and a TV stand is just one more piece of furniture to dust. I would highly recommend getting Roku TVs, as their remotes are very user-friendly and you will get fewer questions about them.

We do not provide satellite or cable TV in most of our homes. Most guests are happy to just sign into their streaming service like they would at home. Most sports fanatics have their login credentials to watch the big game remotely, so providing a smart TV is usually enough. It could make sense on large or high-end properties to provide cable service, but we have not noticed much of a perceived value from the guests and have eliminated the overhead in most of our homes. It may also be worth considering if you need something to differentiate your listing in an urban market or if you are in a rural market and do not have fast enough internet to allow for streaming.

Projectors are often a bit complicated, so unless you have a legitimate theater room and need a projector, I would just buy a large smart TV. If you do have a projector, make sure to give clear instructions on how to operate it.

Locks: Having a digital front door lock is definitely the way to go in most situations, but they are not trouble-free. Many guests are still intimidated and confused by digital keypads, and many manufacturers still don't make a user-friendly product. We have eight different brands of digital locks on our properties, but our favorite brand is probably Schlage. Do not buy a digital lock that does not have a physical backup key. We keep an old-fashioned emergency lockbox by the front door with the backup key, and the lockbox is labeled with our phone number so they can call for the code if the lock fails or they just can't figure it out.

Make sure you give specific instructions regarding the lock in your checking message. If the guest has to tap the keypad to wake up the screen or has to press the pound button after their code, make sure that is in the guest message. We also label the lock itself with any specific instructions using a label maker.

Unless the digital lock that you use shows battery life remaining in your lock and is accurate, you need some type of system for routinely changing batteries in the lock.

Some brands will die without any warning, which can cause a crisis situation at check-in.

Cameras: All cameras must be disclosed in the listing and should never be inside the home or facing an area outside where guests should reasonably expect privacy.

Cameras can be a useful tool, but they can also drive you crazy if you have notifications turned on your phone and are bothered by knowing what is going on at your property. Some people do not have the personality to not check the camera or ignore what guests are doing. If your guest says they are bringing four guests, but there are six cars in the driveway, are you going to confront them? If they are carrying case after case of beer into the house, are you going to say anything or not unless you see them exceed the guest count?

Cameras are helpful for several things, including seeing if a guest arrives early or late or if they bring a pet without disclosing that or paying the pet fee. However, lots of things that the camera reveals are difficult to accuse the guest of without coming across as invasive. If you notice a pet as they walk in from their car, it is better to say after the reservation that the cleaner noticed pet hair or something of that nature and ask if they had brought a pet. Confronting them during the reservation based on you watching them in the driveway is disturbing, and it makes them uncomfortable for the rest of their stay and will probably not have a great impact on their review.

Noise sensors: A noise monitoring system such as NoiseAware or Minut is very beneficial in certain situations. NoiseAware is able to monitor the decibels in the house without picking up on or transmitting the actual noise, so guests maintain privacy, but the host can monitor if things are getting too loud. We have used it in the past but have found it to be inconsistent with our Wi-Fi and a bit expensive for the value that we got from it. These softwares are very popular now and can automatically message guests a warning if they break a sound threshold, so long as they are compatible with your PMS. Some of these software programs even offer features like cigarette detection.

Speakers and Bluetooth: We do not provide speakers or a Bluetooth radio in any of our homes. Providing any type of speaker or sound system seems like it would encourage guests to be loud and get complaints from neighbors. If you are dead set on having a system, I will have it fixed so it cannot be brought outside unless you have no neighbors for miles around.

HOUSEHOLD GOODS

To make your guests feel at home, you need to provide the creature comforts one normally uses at home. These items can add up quickly, and most of them should be purchased in the lower to mid-end range.

Coffee Pot: We provide both a standard 12-cup drip coffee pot and Keurig in each unit, and we provide the coffee grounds and K cups for each. I highly recommend not getting a combination unit that has both a drip coffee pot and Keurig, because

when one dies, you have to replace the whole unit. Broken coffee pots are also pretty common, so you don't want to have to try to find a replacement pot to save a $150 unit; you just want to put in a new

$30 coffee pot in the unit. We buy the name brand Keurig (basic model for about $60) and about a $30 stainless steel but pretty basic 12 cup coffee maker. Sometimes the ultra-cheap coffee pots don't have the auto-off function, so a guest can leave the coffee pot for days, so make sure you check that before buying.

Hair dryer: We provide a basic hair dryer in every home, usually multiple in large homes. We don't provide any other hair products or feminine products, but that is not a bad idea if you want to go the extra mile.

Soap Dispensers: You want your soap dispensers to be see-through and large, at 12–16 ounces. If it is opaque, your cleaners will not be able to visually check it and will miss it fairly often. We use the mason jar style and buy them on Amazon. We also use a soap dispenser for our Dawn Dish Soap in the kitchen sink instead of the plastic bottles.

High Chair and Pack n Play: These are both great for larger homes that tend to have family gatherings and are traveling a distance. If you have space in a bedroom, a crib is a great option as well.

Towel holders: Guests are rough on towel holders; whether it is a hand towel holder or a bath towel bar or toilet paper holder, it will get ripped out of the wall unless both ends are anchored into a stud. No towel bar is set to the standard 16-inch stud spacing, which means you end up with a drywall anchor on one side that will get ripped out. To avoid this, we mount the towel rod onto a 1x6 and screw the 1x6 to the wall on the studs. If you are going for rustic decor, black iron pipe is a good option for a bath towel holder, as it is nearly unbreakable. If you can't get a toilet paper holder or a hand towel holder on the stud, just go with a free-standing option.

Fire Extinguisher: The best practice is to have one fire extinguisher per floor, mounted in a visible place. This may be required by your short-term rental ordinance, or they may have specific requirements as to the type and capacity of the fire extinguisher. If you have a wood-burning fireplace, it is a good idea to mount one near that as well.

First Aid Kit: We keep a basic first aid kit at every property and store it under the kitchen sink so we know where to tell guests to look if they ask. It doesn't have to be anything extravagant, but it shows guests that you care when their kids scrape their knees, and most will see it when they look under the kitchen sink to get the dishwasher pods, so whether they use it or not, it helps you look prepared. We check the kit during our monthly checks, but it rarely gets used.

Lamps: Lamps often give us trouble, and they commonly get unplugged by guests who want to use the outlet to charge their phone. Many lamps now come with a USB port built in, which is ideal, and some end tables and bedside tables have them built in as well. Your lamps should be very user-friendly; there should be no confusing switches or touch pads to turn them on. They should also be fairly durable, and the shades should not be intricate or hard to clean.

Curtains and Blinds: With a few exceptions, curtains are by far the better choice when compared to blinds. Blinds get broken all the time, especially mini blinds. Think about it: something controlled by a string and pulled by a bunch of kids and drunk adults who are not used to those specific blinds. Some blinds now don't have chords, and how these magically window covers are supposed to operate is not self-evident to many guests who try to force them up and down and end up breaking them. Two-inch blinds seem to be a little bit more durable, but they are much more expensive and still get broken. Paper blinds are an absolute nightmare.

The best option is to go with a thermal-backed curtain with a durable curtain rod mounted into studs. No, the drywall anchors will not hold. If you go this route, you can go years without having to worry about them, and the energy efficiency from the thermal backing is significant if you have older windows. For high windows and windows that don't have a privacy issue, consider skipping curtains altogether.

Cleaning Accessories: Your cleaner should be providing the supplies and equipment for them to do their job, but you still want to leave the basic cleaning supplies available to the guest so they can clean up after themselves. This includes basic sprays and sponges, a broom and dustpan, a mop, and a vacuum if you have any rugs or carpet. For the vacuum, we just recommend a basic bagless corded vacuum. Don't try to get cute with any battery-operated stuff because a guest will never plug it in and the battery will always be dead. Guests will also never clean out the vacuum, so make sure your cleaner or property manager is emptying the vacuum and cleaning its filters. We are experimenting with leaving a robot vacuum on site for guests to use, hoping that it might encourage them to leave the place a little cleaner.

Before we close the section on household goods, I want to mention a few things we do not provide. We don't provide a toothbrush holder or a bar soap holder for the bathroom because they get gross and are hard to clean. We also don't provide hampers or laundry baskets for the guests to use, as we have not gotten feedback requesting them, and guests are going to leave their towels wherever they want anyway. Even if we provide a desk or designated work space, we don't provide a printer, because that seems like a nightmare, and as we are not in a market with a lot of business travel, we don't get that request. We also don't provide air freshener sprays or plug-ins. We don't provide an emergency toothbrush or toothpaste, Q-tips, or anything of that nature, though if you want to go above and beyond those, those are not bad touches.

Kitchen Supplies: Which cooking supplies you provide in the kitchen is wildly dependent on your kitchen, market, and customer avatar, but it usually doesn't pay to skimp out or not provide what guests might expect at their price point or for the size of the home. If the home can accommodate a large group, they will expect to cook for a large group.

We usually purchase everything a guest could reasonably expect to need, but we stay on the cheaper end of the scale for most products. We don't buy expensive silverware or utensils, as they get lost, broken, and abused, and they don't add a lot of perceived value. We've never gotten a good review that said "Awesome silverware, five-star home" or a bad review that said "their measuring cups were really cheap; I would not recommend this home."

One place we do spend a little more for quality is on a nice stainless steel cookware set, and we avoid Teflon pots or pans. Some bozo will not put cooking oil in the pan, and another lamebrain will scrape it off with a knife and wreck the Teflon. Some guests are concerned about scratched Teflon these days, so it is generally advisable to just spend the extra money and get a nice stainless steel set. We use the Duxtop brand that you can find on Amazon, and they have great reviews and are on the lower cost side for quality stainless steel sets.

Decor:

It's often said, "What catches the eye catches the dollar." This simple truth is why it's important to make your listing stand out in the sea of other short-term rentals.

The majority of potential guests scanning through listings look at photos first, and if you can't catch their attention, they will never look at your reviews, listing description, or price; they will move on to something that will actually catch their attention.

And yet, common sense dictates that a lot of decor looks nice but is just not practical in a rental space. I often see antiques and decor I would love to put in a cabin, but I know that a child will break it within a week, so aesthetics has to be balanced with practicality. Also, 65%–70% of bookings (in our market) are by females. Keep this in mind when choosing decor and thinking about who you are marketing towards.

Decor is not my strong suit, and I don't pretend to be an expert, so I will just share a few thoughts and tricks that I believe in. As a general principle, you want the decor and theme of your house to have a fairly broad appeal and not be too specific, unless you are in a saturated market and need to do something bold to stand out. Get a simple color scheme and have consistent tones and "vibes" throughout your space. It is generally ok to be a little more bold with your colors and themes in bedrooms, and this is much safer than using wild colors and themes in common areas. Having different themes in bedrooms is especially helpful in differentiating between rooms in the listing. If you have a six-bedroom house, don't paint all six bedrooms the same gray color and put the same bedspread on the same queen bed. Diversity maintains interest.

We are in the cabin and rustic market here in North Georgia and tend to keep it simple with country decor and often white walls in our cabin. Flat white paint is easy to touch up but can make everything look a little bland if you don't have some colorful decor and nice features in the home to liven things up. Faux plants are a good touch to add some greenery, but for the love of donuts, don't make your cleaners keep live plants alive. Area rugs, although a little more work for your cleaners and more expense for you, will soften up the space and are great for bedrooms and living rooms. Don't put an area rug under the dining room table, as that is a disaster waiting to happen. We like mirrors a lot, as they double as both decor and utility. Most humans like to look at themselves a lot, and as we are in a wedding market, they often appreciate full-length mirrors for getting ready.

Maintain good lighting in every room. Lamps help fill a space and add needed light to rooms that don't have quite natural light or too many dark colors. Make sure you stick with the same color temperature for all light bulbs. There is nothing more frustrating than going to replace light bulbs and having some cool white and some bright light bulbs in the same chandelier. Be mindful of things that could offend a moderate percentage of guests. It's impossible to not offend anyone, but you want the space approved for general audiences. Pictures that have nudity may be art, but they are also offensive to a fairly broad group of people. Deer heads may be great in a hunting lodge, but in some circumstances, they will turn off other potential guests. It's also important not to have too much personalization; we would not recommend family photos or things that would make people feel like they are strangers in someone else's home. The goal is to make it feel like their private home away from home.

Overall, I would be cautious about overspending on decor. Don't hear what I'm not saying; you don't want your decor items to look or feel cheap. You don't want your guests to walk in and know that you have everything on Facebook Marketplace. But you also don't always get the value that you pay for when you spend the big bucks on your decor. There is a human tendency to be too opinionated as to what you think looks good and is worth paying for. I see this as a common area to overspend on for those who have a passion for decorating. It's as if they say, "What? I get to spend money to decorate, and it's a tax write-off? Sky's the limit!" If you want to be in the game long-term, you have to treat your rental like a business and keep your hobbies separate. If you just have to spend more on decor, furnishings, and additional welcome gifts, you are, of course, welcome to do so. Some people would rather operate off of their personal preference than make a few extra grand a year. I get that; I just don't get it. I will paint all the walls pink with purple polka dots if that is what has the broadest appeal—it's not my personal home, and I can separate "church and state" in my mind.

It is also important not to put out anything that is sentimental or irreplaceable. If you have a portrait that your grandmother painted and you have no space to hang it in your personal home, hanging it in your rental is not the solution. Decor doesn't get broken that often, but never roll the dice on something that is sentimental. If it's irreplaceable, it's irreplaceable.

Another nice touch is to try to use interactive items to decorate your space.

If you can come up with decor that's a conversation piece, good to fiddle with, or interactive; it's a win-win. Some examples of these are Jenga, hourglasses, balancing toys, abacuses, magnetic stones, or balancing blocks. One thing within the category that we would generally not recommend would be candles. While they are typically not the end of the world if they get put out or used at a rental, all it takes is one irresponsible guest to burn something or spill wax all over the table.

The final word of caution on decor is to pay attention to the right volume or quantity of decor.

Both bare walls and cluttered shelves are more common than they should be. Every large section of wall should have something on it, and no shelf should be left completely bare, but you also have to take into consideration the time it will take to dust and properly clean all the decor. You don't want to end up with a higher cleaning fee because of the labor it will take to dust all those knickknacks or clean all those books and toys.

Linens:

Linens are a topic that is highly debated, and many people are strongly opinionated about the absolute right strategy. I don't expect my take on what is best to be widely accepted, but our market is a little bit different than urban markets. We stay away from white as much as possible. This includes, but is not limited to, sheets, comforters, bath mats, rugs, washcloths, and towels. There are several reasons for this. First, our cabins in the woods are surrounded by dirt and clay, which are a fatal blow for white sheets. Every time a guest gets clay, makeup, or wine on those pretty white sheets, you have the option of fighting with them over the cost, risking a bad review, or just eating the cost.

White linens also require that your cleaners use bleach with their laundry, which is bad for septic systems. Although I agree that clean white linens are a great look, they are just not practical for our market. We typically use something in the gray or brown family of colors for sheets and comforters. This doesn't mean everything has to be boring, and there are several nature-themed prints on comforters to keep things looking interesting.

For comforters, we typically go with something thinner and lighter and have additional blankets and comforters in the closets or at the foot of the bed if guests get cold. I believe it's better to do it this way, especially if you're doing laundry on site, as a thick comforter is hard on your washing machine if it will fit in at all. In our market, most of the cleaners wash on site, and if they do take linens off site, you need a process to track them or inventory them so things don't go missing. Many hosts use duvet covers, but we have found them frustrating and usually just stick with a simple quilt or comforter.

Keep one spare set of sheets for each bed. I would also have a minimum of one spare comforter per size of bed, preferably one per bed. Queen and full-size linens get mixed up all the time, so if you have both, clearly label your sheets. King sheets are also frustrating to orient as the length and width are only two inches different, so it's helpful to have a pattern to help cleaners figure out what's on the head and what's on the side of the sheet. An alternative to this is to just label the tag with an arrow if the tag isn't already labeled head or foot, as many smart manufacturers are already doing.

Towels often do not have a long lifespan in short-term rentals, and unless you have a small, luxury property, I don't see where it would make sense to buy expensive towels; there is too high of a risk of them getting ruined. Again, we don't do white because of the dirt and clay in these hills, but especially because of our hot tubs. Even if we provide towels specifically for outdoor use, bath towels will still go out to the hot tub. Some local hosts do white towels and provide the black makeup towels, but I don't think the specific makeup towel significantly reduces the staining on your white towels.

If you have a pool or hot tub, provide pool towels to reduce the use of your bath towels outdoors. The best way to do this is to put a bin of them near the door leading to the hot tub or pool. Make sure your guests have plenty of towels and that they don't have to wash towels on a three- or four-night stay. Our rule of thumb for a regular home without a hot tub or pool is at least two bath towels per guest for the maximum occupancy of the house, with others available if the guest requests them.

It is also important to do a quality check on your linens. Many cleaners get blinded to the quality of what they are putting out; they are looking for cleanliness and stains, but if a towel is becoming thin and rough, they don't notice it. We do a quality check on towels on our three-month inspections.

Bathmats: We typically have one bath mat per bathroom, with one or two backups available for the cleaners on site. They typically don't need to be large, and the larger the mat, the harder it is on your washer and dryer. We don't do the around the toilet mat or toilet seat cover as that is a cleanliness issue, and then you have to match everything in the set when it is time to replace one piece. Make sure your cleaners are routinely washing the bathmats and flagging them for replacement as needed.

Supplies: Supplies, or "consumables", are an ongoing expense that must be well monitored and executed. I suppose that supplies that guests expect in the home will vary based on the market and price point of the property, but I will outline the standard supplies that we put in our units, as most of them correlate to all markets. Before we get into the specific supplies, it's important to know that the size and quality of the consumables are very important, and finding a good wholesale price without having a storage issue is a careful balance. We buy our supplies wholesale and pass them on to our owners at our expense. We try to buy in quantities large enough to get the price down wherever applicable, but we have a lot of storage space that you likely won't have in your home. Some stores, like Walmart, won't give any price breaks based on quantity but are still the cheapest, while others will give a significant price break at a reasonable quantity. If the items are small and easy to store and you get a significant break, you can justify tying up some cash, but you don't have thousands of dollars of supplies on hand just to save a couple bucks in discounts. The other component to purchasing is the time it takes; you don't want to have to place an order every week for supplies for your rental, so you have to factor in time, discounts, storage, and quantity price savings into your strategy. We have thousands of items in stock at our office and well north of ten thousand dollars in inventory, but to me, it's worth tying up some cash to get the price down and not having to be ordering things every day.

These are the supplies we put in our homes, listed in alphabetical order with a couple notes if I deem them helpful. We inventory our supply closets monthly to make sure we have a sufficient backup of these on site. We don't check how much salt is left in the salt shaker every month; we just ensure that there is a new salt container in storage that the cleaning crew can pull from to refill the salt shaker. This is the simplest way to ensure you don't have to scramble to get something to a

cleaner or guest. Your supply closet needs to be well organized and laid out. We straighten up our supply closet as the first step to doing an inventory. If you can't stand in one spot and see all of the items on your checklist, that means neither can the cleaner, and they are going to text you they are out of hand soap when they are not because it is under the backup comforter that got jammed in the supply closet.

- Ant baits: You may or may not use professional pest control, but they are good to keep on hand to be put out preventatively or at the first sign of problems.
- Batteries (9v, AA, AAA): Need some on hand so that the chirping smoke detector or

remote battery doesn't turn a small issue into a large one.

- Wasp Spray
- Coffee (ground and K-cups)—we provide an adequate amount of both. This is one of our most commonly asked questions before a guest stays.
- Coffee Filters
- Dishwasher Pods: We used to use dishwasher liquid, but the pods ended up being both more guest-friendly and a little bit cheaper per use, as they included the jet dryer, which meant we no longer had to stock that item.
- Grill/Oven Cleaner: You need a degreaser on hand to assist guests and cleaners with cleaning the oven.
- Kitchen Sponges
- Laundry Detergent: We buy a twenty-pound bucket of Arm and Hammer for the plastic bin, then refill it with Tough Guy laundry soap, which we buy in 50-pound boxes. Make sure it is visible to the guest.
- Light Bulbs: Stock every type of bulb that is in the house.
- Lighters

PHYSICAL PRODUCTS

- Paper Towels: We put out one roll per stay, but if there is a partial roll out, we will stick a full roll beside it.
- Pepper
- Propane Tank (spare)
- Roach Bait
- Root Killer (for septic systems)
- Salt
- Salt and Pepper Shaker
- Septic Flush: Septic treatment packs; we flush one monthly.
- Soap, Bar (for showers), individually wrapped,. 5 or 1 oz. size
- Soap, Dish: Don't be cheap; use Dawn. Do everything you can to help guests clean the dishes.
- Soap, Hand
- Toilet Paper
- Towel, Bath
- Towel, Hand
- Towel, Kitchen
- Trash bags, 13 gallon
- Trash bags, Bathroom
- Washcloths

We do not provide tissues or shampoo. I don't think either of these are wrong to provide; it's just not worth it for us at this time. Surprisingly, we don't get any complaints or requests about not having tissues on hand. Is it a nice touch? Of course, but it's not going to move the needle or get you a higher or lower review, and it's one more consumable to purchase and track. We do occasionally get a complaint about not having shampoo, even though we disclose it in our listing that we do not provide shampoo. However, individual-sized shampoos are expensive, and although we have never used them, it is highly likely guests will break the seal on them or use a fraction of the amount, making them unusable for the next guest. A standard shampoo bottle does not seem sanitary, which leaves us without providing shampoo. We get private feedback from about one in every 200 stays saying it would be nice to have shampoo, but nothing in a public review or serious enough to make us change our mind yet. It is important to listen to your guests and adjust to what people expect.

We used to not provide paper towels, and despite disclosing that, we got a lot of complaints about it and even one or two negative public reviews, which caused us to change policies and start providing them. Unfortunately, you pretty much have to provide what people will complain about.

Cleaning supplies: If you are going to be providing cleaning tools and supplies for your cleaner to use at your rental, this is the basic cleaning kit and the minimum items we provide for our cleaners. In most cases, they will provide their own kit, but if you are doing it yourself or hiring your neighbor by the hour, consider supplying the following:

- Hot Tub Skimmer
- Hot Tub Vacuum
- Laundry bags (dirty and clean)
- Corded Vacuum
- Cordless Hand Vac
- Mop, bucket, or pads
- Broom and dustpan
- Microfiber clothes
- Paper Towels
- Disinfectant
- All-purpose cleaner
- Spray bottles (glass cleaner/dawn, multi-surface cleaner)
- Caddy
- Sos/Green Scour Pad
- Magic Erasers

- Toilet Seals
- Scraper
- Toilet Bowl Cleaner
- Stainless steel cleaner
- Dusting Kit with Extension Rod
- Fabric stain removal
- Oven Degreaser

That concludes the very basics you should consider for physical products in your home. I hope that will save you some time in the research process and in the learning curve you will face for your home, but take your time in the planning and execution of what actually goes in your home, because what guests touch and use is a high-impact area for their overall experience.

CHAPTER 10

REVIEW RESPONSES AND REVIEW MANAGEMENT

Mastering the review process takes some experience in order to effectively prevent and respond to negative reviews. I hope the following chapter will shortcut you a few hundred transactions and make you better at the review game right off the bat.

Reviews are serious and should be treated as such, but they are not the end of the world and should not stress you out and make you a miserable person. When I first started hosting, a four-star review would put me in a foul mood for quite a while. I think part of that is good; it means you really care and means you really want an excellent rating to reflect the superior product and service that you provide, but it often is a pride thing, and it feels as if someone has insulted you personally. Now, when we get dinged in a review, I usually have a flare of anger, but it subsides much more quickly than it used to.

The first step in review management is to work hard to get a volume of good reviews and be proactive to avoid upset guests leaving a bad review. The entire book up to this point is about how to build a superior product and service, and if you execute well, you won't get a volume of bad reviews.

One thing that we do, which I theorize helps a lot with reviews but can't prove it, is provide multiple avenues for feedback from guests prior to the review process. We leave paper copies of feedback surveys on site, hoping guests will tell us what we

need to know and also so they will hopefully vent on paper and not in a public review. We take all feedback seriously, and if they fill out this form and say they have an issue, we will shoot them a message apologizing and thanking them for the feedback, so they don't feel they need to also put it in a public review. We also send a digital version of this survey to guests after checkout, again hoping that any complaints they put in the digital survey will appease their desire to complain. Some people won't fill out any surveys; some will fill out both a paper survey and a digital one, but the main thing is to give them an avenue other than the public review to let you know about their stay.

After a guest checks out, message them, let them know you appreciate their business, and thank them for leaving the house in good condition. Unless they were horrific guests, we sent this message. We have this automated message set up, and we just turn it off if we get a bad feeling about the guests or if the cleaners report an issue.

Make sure in this message that you tell them you will be or have given them a five-star review, so that there is reassurance that everything is great on your end and so that they will feel bad if they don't reciprocate a good review. We also ask them to message us with any private feedback about their stay if they didn't have a five-star experience. Don't be overly pushy in requesting a review, and don't ask for a review from a guest with whom you do not have a good relationship. We turn off all automated messages and surveys for guests that we know are unhappy, hoping they forget about us as much as we want to forget about them.

Reviewing good guests is not difficult; it just takes a lot of work if you don't have software that can handle this for you. Fortunately, our PMS automates it for Airbnb, which reduces our work load. For Vrbo, we have a document of generic responses that we copy and paste from so that we can change things up and so that the task does not take forever. Responding to positive reviews is also a significant amount of work if you are doing a volume of transactions or have multiple properties, and there is no automation for this and probably will never be as you often have to craft a specific reply to whatever the guest said. I recommend the same system of writing out 5 or 10 variations and copying and pasting review responses once a week. If someone is looking at your reviews, you don't want every single response to be the same, or you will look like a careless robot. On booking.com, you do not have the ability to review a guest, and you can only respond to a review if they leave written feedback. Booking.com also allows guests to post a picture in their review, but you can't see it from the host end and don't get a notification that they posted a picture, so if you get a negative review, check your listing on the guest-facing side of the site and see if there is a photo that you need to address.

Reviewing bad guests is another tricky part of the process. If I were an individual host, I would not hesitate to give a bad guest a low rating, but with so many retaliatory and vindictive people out there now, we don't often give a guest a bad rating because they can upset and attack us on our Google profile or social media. To be honest, it does very little besides upset the guest because most hosts now have the instant booking option turned on across all platforms, so that guest is going to be able to continue to book properties regardless. You can help out other hosts by giving a bad rating to a guest so they have a heads up that there might be trouble, but it does very little otherwise. Also, because poor ratings are so rare, we very commonly get bad guests with perfect five-star ratings from previous hosts. All ratings should be taken with a grain of salt, as it is often group travel, and sometimes another person in the booking guest group was the one that caused trouble on a previous stay. When we do get a booking from a guest with a low rating and they have specific feedback in a review saying they snuck in a pet or something like that, we do ask the guest about it to put them on notice that we are aware of their rating and won't tolerate any funny business.

You must be proactive in making sure your property is up to par, but also very active in conflict resolution if you get any sense that the guest is not happy. Roughly half the time we get a bad review, we know it's coming and can often make a gesture to reduce the risk, but on the other half of them, the guest never expressed their complaints, and you will not know you are about to get hit. Sometimes you have to swallow your pride and offer freebies or refunds to guests to put them back in your good graces, even if nothing significant went wrong during their stay. It all depends on the guest and their attitude towards inconveniences. I have had guests pay a thousand dollars a night for a nice rental and be very chill and not ask for a dime when the septic system backed up on them and created serious issues. I have also had guests see a couple of spiders and want a refund. There is a risk element in play here, and we do not give large refunds every time to reduce the chances of receiving a low rating. Properties that don't have a lot of reviews, properties that don't have a rating as high as you would like, or bookings on a specific OTA that you really need a good review on may cause you to refund more than you really should have to. There is safety in numbers, so work hard in the first couple of years of your rental to collect lots of five-star reviews on every major OTA, so you don't have to worry about one bad review tanking your score. If you are going to give a refund for an issue or perceived issue, be careful not to issue an insultingly low amount, as this can backfire and actually make the guest more upset.

Whatever you choose to do, be proactive and make sure you are coming across as friendly on an individual level. They are reviewing you as much as the property, so if you are perceived as being rude or unsympathetic, they will really want to stick with you, but if you are super friendly, they will hesitate before being nasty in the review. We do have some good luck offering early check-in or late checkout or waiving a pet fee for minor issues.

If a negative review gets posted, to some degree you are in a lose-lose situation in your review response. If you refute the guest's review, you can come across as argumentative in the eyes of future guests, but if you don't refute it, they may assume that the review is justified. Yet a bad review is not the end of the world, especially if you have a perfectly good and professional response to the review. It is often harder to respond to a review that makes general complaints, like the house being unclean or the management being unfriendly, than it is about one specific issue, like ants in the house.

Respond to every review, and respond to every review as soon as possible. The only time we don't respond to a review in a timely manner is if we are fixing an issue they complained about, so that we can honestly say in the review response that we have fixed the issue. If you only respond to negative reviews, it will make that negative review stand out even more. Airbnb doesn't show the rating of the review, so someone just skimming through the reviews may not even notice the bad review, unless that is the only one you wrote a one-paragraph response to.

Here are some principles that we have in our employee handbook in regards to responding to bad reviews:

- For reviews with less than 5 stars but mostly positive things, generally only acknowledge positive things unless the negative comment is serious and has to be addressed. Don't draw more attention to the negative, as most review readers just skim and will likely miss it.
- Respond to any significant complaint you have a good answer to or have.
- All negative review responses require one other person to check your response before submitting.

- Keep it short; only address what they address; address only serious items if they have a long list of them. The rule of thumb is two sentences of response, or up to half of the length of their review, whichever is shorter.
- It is okay to correct them if they complain about things that were disclosed in the listing that they just didn't read.
- If it's a slightly negative review without a major complaint, don't address it all; just leave a generic response, like "Thanks for staying with us."

Don't have too defensive of a mindset when you get a bad review, and realize that sometimes you do deserve it because you messed up in some way. Whether or not you deserve to be taken down, use it as an opportunity to learn and improve your customer service or your property. Our standard policy is to do an "autopsy" after we receive any review that is not a five-star review and re-read the thread with the guest that left us a bad review to see if we can discover any hints that the guest wasn't happy or any mistakes that we may have made in how we handled a concern. Many times there is no communication with the guest at all;

they just didn't like something about the property or had a complaint they never told you about or gave you a chance to address, but occasionally you will pick up on a clue that you missed when you reread their messages within the context of a bad review.

Occasionally, all hosts will get unfair reviews written about their property.

Sometimes the OTA will take them down, but unless they clearly violate the review policy of that OTA, they will not be taken down. Fortunately, very angry guests often do not know the review policy and will write vindictive reviews that you can get removed. If you charge a guest for breaking an item and they complain about that charge in the review, you can most likely get the OTA to take it down, but if they don't mention that specifically and just give a bad rating, the review won't be taken down.

Never tell a guest on or off the platform that you will give them a refund or waive a fee in exchange for a good review, or in exchange for not leaving a bad review. This is a surefire method to get your listing flagged and possibly get kicked off the platform.

REVIEW RESPONSES AND REVIEW MANAGEMENT

There are several companies out there now that offer the service of review removal, on Airbnb, on Google, etc. We get repeated calls from one of them who says they have someone inside Airbnb that will remove reviews for $100 a piece, and we don't have to pay until the review is taken down. Even if I didn't have an ethical problem with cheating the system like that, it would not be worth the risk of Airbnb finding out and suspending our account.

Because of all of the drama surrounding reviews, it is very convenient to have a direct booking website where guests can't leave reviews. Reviews are important, and many platforms like ours allow you to import reviews to your direct booking website, but they don't have a direct review process. This is one channel where we get some relief from worrying about whether or not we should refund a guest $100 for a minor inconvenience.

So what is a good rating, and what should you be shooting for? Check your market data on AirDNA and see what the average review rating is in your area. In our local market, professional management companies are lower than the average rating. Our rating on Airbnb is currently 4.91, but Evolve's is 4.84 and Vacasa's is a whopping 4.26. The market average is 4.87. This doesn't necessarily mean that management companies are worse than DIY hosts, as I theorize that travelers are more comfortable being critical of companies than individual hosts. Evolve's hybrid model means that the owners are heavily involved in the process and still help create a good product. Our magic number is 4.9, and we aim to keep our overall rating and our individual scores on Airbnb, such as the cleanliness rating, at or above this mark. Maintaining a perfect 5.0 rating is nearly impossible, though we have gotten as many as 60 five-star reviews in a row before getting a four-star review, and some of our properties stay as high as 4.98. I do believe, though I can't prove it, that there are a lot of hosts out there that are more obsessed with their rating than making cash and giving more refunds, as well as providing more hosting gifts and expensive perks to keep their rating near perfect.

Review ratings can get overemphasized, and we do have several properties at a lower price point that we just can't keep a 4.9 rating at, and yet they still book. Some properties are just not 5-star, and even if your listing copy and photos paint an accurate picture, some guests are a little disappointed when they get on site and will withhold the 5-star

REVIEW RESPONSES AND REVIEW
MANAGEMENT

review. Properties at 4.75 and 4.8 will still get reservations; they just stress me out when they get to that range because I know a couple of grumpy guests giving a two-star rating will drop it to the 4.6 range, which is completely unacceptable. I personally would not book anything under a 4.5 unless the property only had a handful of reviews and they had a perfectly good response to their one or two bad reviews.

At the end of the day, reviews are a critical component of the overall success of your rental. Take them seriously and make adjustments to any significant feedback you get from your guests, but don't sweat the small stuff, or you will never stop sweating.

CHAPTER 11

INSURANCE, PERMITS, LIABILITY REDUCTION, AND OTHER FUN STUFF

To reduce my liability, I should once again remind you that you should do your own research and check with a professional in regards to all the legal considerations we will discuss in the chapter. I speak from experience here, but not as a professional, so hire a professional or put in the work to figure out what you need to do to make sure you operate legally, safely, and within the risk tolerance you are comfortable with.

Most of this book is about offense, how to make a great product, and how to generate money. But it's important to pause for a second and think defensively, to contemplate how you can avoid losing everything you have worked your tail off for due to one slip-up. Here are the strategies to reduce your liability that we will discuss:

- Only operate a STR with a valid license or licenses and stay up-to-date on all local rules.

INSURANCE, PERMITS, LIABILITY REDUCTION, AND OTHER FUN STUFF

- Have sufficient insurance.
- Have your property in an LLC or separate legal entity from your personal assets.
- Don't hire incompetent people.
- Have proper signage on site.

We start off with valid licensing, as there is no point in going any further in the process if you cannot secure a valid short-term rental license. Ensuring that you can attain a license is the first thing you check when considering a property, and you should absolutely not close on a property unless you are positive you are in the clear. I would not even waste time doing my due diligence on the property itself and putting in an offer if it didn't have a clear path to licensure. Pick up the phone, call the local government office that is responsible for licenses, give them the address, and make sure there are no roadblocks. If the property is in a subdivision, get the most updated copy of the covenants and make sure there are no restrictions. If there are other short-term rentals in the neighborhood, try to get a hold of those owners or property managers and ask them if they have received any pushback from the HOA or any of the full-time residents. Some communities have many short-term rentals and are friendly towards them;

others hate them but just can't organize enough to actually change the covenants and get them outlawed.

When you are on the phone with the local government, ask them to walk you through the process of getting a license and all the requirements, and also get them to email you a copy of the application packet and any other information that might be helpful. You can also ask them for recommendations for local management companies, which they may or may not be allowed to give you. Make sure you ask them specifically about tax remittance, if there is anything you would need to do for that, and what the tax rate is to set up for your listings. If you are going to be taking direct bookings, most likely you will need to get a tax account with the state and figure out how to remit taxes yourself.

The local government may have property inspections in order to attain and maintain a valid license, so make sure you have a list of what they inspect and that your property meets those requirements or that the property you are researching is worth updating to those standards. For example, if they require all smoke detectors to be hardwired and interconnected, that is not easy to do without shedding a lot of drywall.

I shouldn't have to say this, but I do. If you can't get a license, don't launch the rental. It's not worth the stress, it's not worth the risk, and it's not worth just paying the HOA fines and running a rental anyway. Setting up your property correctly means a lot of upfront expenses in the setup, and that can't be recouped in a couple of months until you get shut down. Don't be the fool who invests 100 hours of work and $10,000 in furniture and expenses just to get a cease and desist letter from the county. Short-term rentals are a hot topic all across the nation, and most local municipalities have some type of enforcement and complaint line for reporting abuses. Oftentimes, there are significant fines associated with complaints, so if you don't have the right to do it, don't take the risk that comes with being in the wrong.

Homeowner's insurance and liability insurance have changed a lot in the past few years in regards to short-term rentals, much of it for the better. When I first started, there were very few good insurance carriers, and the rates were pretty high. I initially used Proper Insurance, which is a great company, but they are very expensive. Now most major companies will underwrite short-term rentals, and the rates are typically not too far above a standard home insurance policy or a long-term rental policy.

You absolutely must make sure that your policy is written specifically for short-term rentals and that there are no exclusions that you will violate, like renting out your home more than the number of nights a year the policy states. If your insurance does not know you are operating a short-term rental, they can deny you coverage for anything that happens, even if a tree falls on your house when it is vacant. It doesn't pay to not tell the truth; just get the proper coverage. Rates do tend to be all over the place, so just keep calling until you get enough quotes to confirm you are getting a square deal, or get your agent to shop around for you, but don't allow them to just get one quote from their preferred underwriter. Unless you are broke and are running with little cash in the bank (which is not ideal in this business), I would highly recommend keeping a high deductible if it keeps your insurance costs down. If you make a claim, your rates will shoot up for several years following the claim, so it only makes sense to make a claim for serious and significant issues. The odds of a claim of this nature happening are fairly low, and you can usually make up the difference between a low and high deductible in just a couple years of savings from the higher deductible.

A few things at the property that some insurance companies don't like are playground equipment, bunk beds, and missing handrails on exterior stairs. If you have your home already set up and get rejected because of bunk beds, it's your call on whether it is worth changing things up or just telling that company to take a hike.

There are a few other things that insurance companies often miss but are required by building code, and I believe they are necessary to limit your exposure and to just be a responsible human and keep other humans safe. All legal bedrooms must have an egress window with a minimum opening size, usually 5.7 square feet. Do not stick a bed in a basement room without a window and call it a bedroom.

Anything that is high off the ground (typically 30 inches), such as a deck, retaining wall, or staircase inside or outside, must have spindles with maximum spacing requirements. Check your local codes, but it is usually about four inches maximum. If your spacing is too large, a child can fall through. This is a very common problem in our market, as I don't think our county did much of anything for inspections until about fifteen years ago, and people continue to add decks to their property without getting permits or doing things right. Also, make sure you don't have a visual railing that is not an actual structural railing. A screened-in porch must also have spindles, as the screen is not structural.

When you purchase the home, make sure to do your homework with your home inspector and hire someone who doesn't look for nitpicky things, but the important structural things like an unbolted ledger board for your deck. Your insurance appraiser is great at criticizing the age of your roof and pointing out handrails they want, but they either don't know or don't check for things of this nature.

The next step to reducing risk is to put the property in an LLC. If you don't have a lot of equity in the home and don't have many or any personal assets, this may not be necessary, but most people getting into the game have enough personal wealth that it is worth having a separate entity. If you have multiple properties, you may want to consider multiple LLCs, but at some point, it becomes a nightmare to have to track expenses, have a separate set of books, and file taxes for so many different companies. Do not do the work of putting your property into an LLC and then be undisciplined and start commingling expenses, putting some things on your personal credit card, and having sloppy record-keeping. Doing this can open you up to getting personally sued if you can't show a clear and real distinction between you and the business. Get a credit card for the LLC, a separate bank for the LLC, and have a clear separation.

There is a lot of good information out there on finding the structure that is right for you, but for most property owners, an LLC is usually right. Most properties are not held in corporations for specific tax disadvantages, such as double taxation, so make sure you know what you're doing before you shoot yourself in the foot by trying to do something complicated.

After having the insurance and legal structure in place, you now need to make sure you have competent people running the show. If you are not living near the rental, you need to have someone you trust monitoring the property, whether that be a property manager or someone you hire to go through occasionally and handle maintenance and look for liability issues. Remember that some people have a higher risk tolerance than others, and especially so when it's not their rear end on the line. Some bad property managers are lazy or too busy and don't get things repaired, and sometimes they are afraid owners will complain about the expense of getting things fixed or done right. Either way, the best thing you can do is be on site personally at least once or twice a year to make sure that someone with a fresh set of eyes and common sense is noticing that big dead tree leaning towards your house.

It is also important to hire a competent cleaner and handyman and ask them to look for anything that might be dangerous to a guest. This is another way that a budget cleaner can hurt you, or a $15 an hour handyman can really not save you money. If you're talking to him on the phone and he sounds like he could walk into a padded room with two steel balls and lose one and break the other, that's probably not who you want repairing your deck. Not always, but often people who work really cheap are used to working for people who are only trying to keep expenses down and will do things the fast and cheap way, even if it means improper materials or not doing it to code.

To look at the same coin from a positive perspective, a knowledgeable and proactive property manager can be a huge asset if you are not able to be on site regularly. Not only should they be knowledgeable as to what are actually high-risk concerns and what are non-issues, but they should also be on site regularly with the experience to pick up on these things. And most importantly, if their company brand is on the line and their professional insurance policy is at risk, they have significant skin in the game and have good reason to avoid an injury and a lawsuit. I think this is one of the most underappreciated arguments for hiring a property manager. You are effectively cutting your risk in half by having a partner who is responsible for the day to day operations. If negligence is to blame, there is a good chance you will not be the one on the hook for that if you have passed off that responsibility to a property management company.

The final significant measure you can take to reduce liability is to make sure you have proper signage. With the technological advantages of sign and printing industry, you can get custom warning signs made fairly inexpensively for your rental. You don't want to overwhelm your space with so many warning signs that you have to put up a sign to beware of signs. Too many signs, and your space will feel commercial and uninviting. You want people to feel unrestricted while on vacation, not like they're in school or under the thumb of their corporate job and following rules, but you do need to cover your butt with a clearly stated warning against anything that could have a reasonable chance of injury. If you find yourself wanting or needing to put up a lot of signs, save your warnings for things that pose a true risk of liability or significant damage to your property. Some examples of these would be pools, hot tubs, uneven steps, low head clearance areas in a stairwell, tripping hazards, doors that need to remain locked, property lines, and areas not suitable for children. From a management perspective, we are trying to limit stupidity in order to keep guests safe and owners happy. It's difficult, actually impossible, to prevent some people from doing absurd things. Usually they're not damaging, just strange, like rearranging furniture and kitchen supplies.

INSURANCE, PERMITS, LIABILITY REDUCTION, AND OTHER FUN STUFF

So how do you post rules and warnings where people will actually read them?

The first rule of thumb is to post the rules as close as possible to the violation. If you're going to post what not to flush down the toilet, do so right next to the toilet, not in the information binder. It is good to reiterate rules and warnings in the information binder, but for anything that poses a significant risk, you want it posted in large print where it can't be ignored.

The next rule of thumb is to make it as short as possible. If you have 36 hot tub rules, they might read three, possibly none. Put the most important item at the top of the list, if there is one. If it isn't critical, or if you haven't had multiple violations, don't even bother saying it because you'll just water down the content that needs to get across.

Use humor as often as possible, so as not to feel controlling. One of our rentals went on a rough streak for the first year, but with some better strategies and warnings, we haven't had these issues in quite some time. This is our list of rules that we have posted in the living room of the rental, trying to make light of some minor issues we've had with guests and the neighbor next door.

INSURANCE, PERMITS, LIABILITY REDUCTION, AND OTHER FUN STUFF

Things we shouldn't need to say but need to say (because people have done all these things):

- If you yell at each other and play loud music at night, the neighbors will complain (People like to sleep at night).
- Do not burn trash in the propane fireplace (It's not real wood, and there is no chimney).
- Do not go across the creek to the neighbor's property and pet their horse. (She is pretty but bites strangers).
- Do not throw beer bottles and Solo cups in the woods (The deer are underage, so don't drink responsibly).
- Do not golf in the field, and especially don't hit golf balls across onto the neighbor's property (There is a golf course in town).
- If you move furniture, put it back (You may have a better arrangement in mind, but my interior designer will be offended).
- The AC will not work when it is below freezing out (If you are really hot when it is freezing out, turn down the heat or crack a window and get that fresh mountain air).

- If you break something or find it broken, please report it (It will not fix itself after you check out).

Thanks, and enjoy your stay!

Tongue-in-cheek sounds friendly and is the only effective way we've come up with to get information across without feeling rude or bossy.

It also goes a long way toward having your signs professionally made—it takes you up a notch in professionalism in the eyes of your guests. Professional signs don't cost an arm and a leg, so just spend a few bucks and get something that looks good and will last. If you really can't afford professional signs, print something that looks nice on cardstock paper and add your logo or a background photo of your property. Whatever you do, don't handwrite anything, like you're the disgruntled employee of a sketchy gas station who doesn't get paid enough to care.

All liability strategies are designed to reduce your chance of an incident as much as possible and then pass the risk off to another party as much as possible. Whether that is the guest having been warned, a property manager being responsible, or an insurance company footing the bill if something unforeseen does happen, you need to spread the risk as much as you can within reason.

CHAPTER 12

INTERVIEWING A PROPERTY MANAGER OR PUTTING TOGETHER YOUR TEAM

As we near the end of the book, I want to draw your attention to something that I have been dancing around the entire book but have not directly addressed, which is the decision to manage a short-term rental yourself or have it professionally managed. My assumption is that most people who picked up this book came into it with one or the other pretty much decided on, and I truly don't intend to change anyone's mind. As the old saying goes, "A man convinced against his will is of the same opinion still."

I hope to offer some advice when interviewing a property manager and give you some questions you can lob at them to get a snapshot of what things would look like if you used their services. We will conclude the chapter with questions to ask the seller of a short-term rental, which should be helpful to many who read this book whether or not they are going to self-manage.

INTERVIEWING A PROPERTY MANAGER
OR PUTTING TOGETHER YOUR TEAM

If at all possible, interview at least three management companies. If you are in a rural market that has not had a significant amount of rentals for a long time, there may not be three management companies, or there may not be three that are worth interviewing. One look at their website and their reviews may eliminate them right off the top. In my neck of the woods, there are some older, very traditional cabin rental companies that have not kept up with industry changes.

Unless you are convinced you will self-manage and already have a cleaner and handyman in place, I would not put in an offer on a property until I had a conversation with a local property manager and had a good feeling about their service. Surprisingly, we normally get a call after someone has a home under contract or has even bought the home. I think people are surprised when they start calling around about how difficult it is to find a reliable property management company. They have heard all the not so true rumors of huge gross numbers and assume there are multiple management companies that have capitalized on it, not realizing how much work the industry actually is and how difficult it is to survive as a STR management company. The vast majority of short-term rentals are managed by individual hosts, so your area may not have the market to support a management company. So do the work and call around and get options before putting in an offer, or you will have nobody to blame but yourself when you get in a bind.

In the past few years, there has been a huge increase in cohosting, and Airbnb promotes this method and makes it very easy to setup, even offering split payouts to cohosts. Cohosting typically has a lower percentage than full-service property management, and it is normative to fall in the 10–20 percent range. Cohosts can be near the subject property or managed remotely, and they can work off of any structure you want, whether it only be customer service or running the majority of the day.

Whichever type of management you are looking for, here is a list of questions that would be wise to ask a property manager, along with a few thoughts on why it matters where applicable.

1. What is your commission rate? The industry average for full service management is anywhere from 20–40%. Don't expect to

pay less than 20% unless your property is cranking out six figures.

2. What is included in that? There is a wide range of services included; get specifics and examples.

3. Will it go down if I make more money or up if I make less, or is it locked?

4. How often can I stay in my rental? Are there any restrictions on peak season?

5. Do I have to pay the cleaning fee after my stay?

6. Do you own short-term rentals yourself? If so, can you tell me a little about them and how they perform? It is a good thing if the manager is also an investor, has experience spending his own money, and has skin in the game and a personal stake in the local market.

7. How many property owners do you work for, and how many properties do you manage? Every manager has to have their first property, but you really don't want to be their first client unless they have been managing a portfolio of their own properties and have experience. If the manager only manages for one person who owns ten

properties, that's not a lot of verification, but if they manage for multiple owners, and if some of those owners have a couple of properties, that is a healthy situation.

8. What is your retention rate or contract renewal rate? Sometimes owners leave the program due to life changes, but the company should have a high retention rate otherwise.

9. How long have you been managing?

10. What are your cleaning reviews like? This is a good question to verify after seeing what they if they say they are great, and then you check Airbnb and see they are a 4.4, they either have a low standard or are not in tune with reality.

11. Do you handle cleaning with employees or cleaning companies?

12. How long have your cleaners been working for you? The cleaning part of the business experiences a high turnover rate; if they have a long-term relationship with vendors or have long-term cleaning employees, this is rare and probably implies they have found some gems and that they are good managers that can deal fairly and keep people happy.

13. What is your staff-to-cabinet ratio? How long have your employees been with you? Some property managers juggle more balls than they can handle and try to manage fifty properties per employee. Being understaffed and having no long-term employees implies they are drowning and will just be too busy, and there is a good chance their staff does not have the experience to do their jobs with excellence.

14. How far do you or your employees live or work from my location? If they are going to be an hour away, you might as well pay a co-host 10% to help you manage it remotely.

15. What is your average review score?

16. How many homes do you manage that are similar to mine? Are they in the same area? A manager can't accurately project income if they don't manage comps.

17. Have you ever been through a slow market? How bad can it get when things get slow?

18. How did your properties do in comparison with other properties during a downturn?

19. Do you think my property would perform better or worse than most in a slow market?

20. Have you ever experienced an awesome market?
21. How did your properties do in comparison with other properties when the market was great?
22. How much is a normal range of fluctuation in gross revenue?
23. What OTAs do you list? If they do not list on every major channel, that is a big red flag.
24. Do you have an owner's portal where I can view reservations?
25. How often will I get statements and payouts?
26. How much do supplies cost, and how are they billed?
27. How are repairs handled, and how do they get billed?
28. How does routine maintenance get handled, and how does it get billed?
29. What would be a range of gross rent, not including taxes and cleaning fees, that my property would bring in, assuming I don't stay in it? You want to take your personal use out of the equation to see what they come back with.

30. How do you handle the setup process?
31. How are photos handled?
32. Are there any additional monthly fees or administrative fees?
33. How can I be certain you are interested in my making a net profit?

A few final thoughts on management before we move on to questioning the seller of a short-term rental. Make sure you are a good fit personally with the manager and reasonably like them and the way they do business. Life is too short to do business with people that you find difficult or who you just don't gel with. I believe this is a lesson everyone has to learn on their own, but maybe some are smarter than me and won't have to learn it the hard way.

Make sure they communicate well; if there is a lack of communication through the sales process, it definitely won't get better when they have your business. Always treat your relationship with your manager like the long-term relationship that it is. It is personal for them too, and you don't want to end up with a strained relationship that you are stuck with. There is a very high switching cost for all parties involved, so you can't just change management companies like you change your socks.

Strangely enough, there is also a subset of people who want a management service but still want to be highly involved in the majority of aspects of their day-to-day lives. It's not realistic to have your cake and eat it too, and if you don't trust the manager to make the right call the majority of the time, they shouldn't be in charge of your property and your wallet. They will make the wrong call occasionally, as it is a difficult business with a lot of variables, and you should give them some grace when they do.

Some people are not mentally at a place where they can hand the keys to someone they don't know very well. That is certainly the case for me, and so I totally get that, and that is the reason I am a property manager and didn't hire one.

If you are going to try to assemble a team and manage yourself from a distance, see Chapter 5 and make sure you can find qualified, local help. It may be a good idea to place a few calls to management companies and find a backup option, just in case the person who is going to be in charge on site decides to back out on you after you have already purchased the property. It is also not a bad idea to have a backup cleaning person just in case your hero gets hit by a bus.

If the desire to do everything yourself is a barrier to entry, I would strongly consider hiring a manager for your first rental. If I had some investment money to spend and was interested in the industry but was too busy to run it day-to-day, I would hire out the management of my first rental as an experiment. If the manager turned out to be excellent and gave me positive cash flow without me putting in much effort, I would keep buying and stay hands-off, but if they were sloppy but the market was good, I would have some data with which to buy additional rentals and take over the management myself. If you make good money on your day job, I just don't think it is worth the bandwidth to manage one rental on the side.

Buying an existing short-term rental

It is a huge advantage to buy a home that is an existing short-term rental, as you will hopefully have some data to work with. A few of these questions will be applicable to any home purchase, but most will not be. The first thing to do if the home is an existing STR is to find the property on

Airbnb or Vrbo and read the reviews. If they are making decent money but marketing and managing their home poorly, this could be a great property for you.

Unfortunately, in today's buying environment, many times real estate agents do not permit you to talk to the buyer directly. If you can talk your way past the agent and get to the source, by all means do so. Some of the questions below are rather direct, but you may have to beat around the bush a little bit and be really nice to the seller in order to get some of this information. You need to get real numbers from the seller, either from the management company they are using or their payout summary from the OTAs they are listed on. Don't trust any numbers they can't prove, and always make sure you are properly assessing those numbers, as they usually include the cleaning fee, and the seller's usually doesn't want to remove

that and would rather pretend the gross number is all rent. Also, make sure you are getting the most current numbers, the last annual year, and if possible, the trailing twelve months, as many rentals are selling because they are down a lot from their 2020 or 2021 highs, and those are the numbers they are bragging about in their listings.

1. What is your cleaning fee, and how much do you pay out to your cleaner? It is possible they are turning a profit on the cleaning fee, and you would want to know that. If the cleaning fee can be lowered, you could increase your occupancy and see a jump in gross revenue. If the cleaning fee is super cheap, that is not a good thing. Sometimes DIY hosts clean it themselves and do it very cheaply, and you could actually have a drop in occupancy if you raise it to the market rate.

2. Is your property now, or has it ever been professionally managed?

3. If your manager knows you are selling the home, can I talk to him about it? Most likely the manager knows, but off-market deals do exist, and if they aren't letting the manager know, there could be contract issues.

4. How would we handle existing bookings that occur after closing? Is the management company contractually due a commission on those reservations?

5. How much gross revenue did it bring in last year and the year before? You want to ask this and verify it to see if they know what is going on and if they are honest.

6. Can you send me a detailed report of your expenses? Jumbled and inaccurate recording keeping are par for the course, but any information you can attain is super helpful.

7. What kind of travelers do you get?

8. Do you get parties?

9. Do you have a good relationship with your neighbors?

10. Have you had any complaints from anyone locally?

11. Do you have a valid STR license?

12. Did you have a hard time getting a license?

13. Are there routine inspections by the local government?

14. Would you be willing to itemize any furniture and household items you are willing to sell so I can choose what works for me?

15. What channels do you list, and how does the home perform on each channel? The best-case scenario is that the homeowner is only listing on one platform and the property is

still performing. If the property is not performing well on a specific channel, check that channel out in detail and see if you can figure out why.

16. Is your cash flow positive, even after all expenses? You should be able to determine if they have a mortgage in public records, but really, this may not matter, as the only thing important to you is if you will be cash flowing with your mortgage or if you are hitting your cash return target if you are paying cash. Many sellers strangely think their home is valuable for bringing in large gross sales when they are at or below break, even after all their expenses. I have talked to many sellers who price with a lot of optimism, basically saying I'm too busy and not really trying, but if someone did more marketing and had time for improvements, they could do a lot better.

Don't' look at a potential property with rose-colored glasses. Take your time to look at how the home is set up and the things that can't be changed or undone. It's like a marriage, at least for those who don't believe in divorce. Once you pull the trigger, you can't undo the purchase; you can't make the location better or the driveway less steep. Scrutinize every property review, fee, and policy in their listing, and think about how things would likely change if you did make changes. Just don't fall into the trap of being an armchair quarterback who assumes that with just a couple of different play calls, they can go from a loser to a winner. There are a lot of variables at play, so unless you are extremely confident, you may just want to buy a base hit with a moderate upside.

CONCLUSION

THE POWER OF A LITTLE BIT

To wrap things up, I would like to illustrate an example of how all the strategies and tips discussed can have a real impact on the year over year net profit. There is no secret sauce or silver bullet to this industry; you just have to be a little bit better in every area and create great systems and small advantages that add up over time. A little bit better here and a little bit better there has a significant cumulative effect. This is not typical of most industries; most industries have a few key performance areas that really move the needle and separate the wheat from the chaff. Short-term rentals have such a broad field that you end up with thousands of little decisions that impact your trajectory along the way.

For illustration purposes, we are going to show numbers on a home that was wisely purchased and properly set up and show how those decisions and the day-to-day operations both contribute to the net result. As I've heard Dave Ramsey say, you make money in real estate on the buy, so if you make a mistake on your purchase, you will be in a world

321 | YOUR NET DETERMINES YOUR NET

of hurt. For this illustration, we are going to assume you made a sound purchase.

Let's say a "nice" 3-bedroom home in a good location will bring in $50,000 per year under normal management in a normal market. Let's say the manager lists Airbnb and Vrbo do an average job but do not go above and beyond. For our market, this is reasonable and within the average range.

First, we will go over the offensive advantages that you create to bring in a higher gross income, and then we will look at the defensive end and see how the savings on expenses will leave you with a higher net. I am trying to use numbers that are realistic for our market and expenses, but please understand that this is an illustration. I am aiming on the conservative side of the numbers, and I think under certain circumstances, these differences could be significantly greater. This is also going to assume experienced management and good local vendors, which you will likely not be able to replicate in the first year or two if you manage yourself and are new to a market.

Baseline "average" rental income: $50,000

Better reviews because of actual, better operations: 2%, $1,000

Using pricing software: 3% more rent, minus cost of software: $1,260

Experience in the local market, setting more accurate pricing: 3%, $1,500

Using booking.com, Google, and a successful direct booking website: 5%, $2,500 Upselling guests for an extra day, 1%, $500

Better amenities, hot tub or game room: 4%, $2,000

Lower cleaning fee because of your design, higher occupancy: 1%, $500

Being pet friendly and doing the work of collecting pet fees: 4%, $2,000

Total Gross Income: $61,260

Competition Gross Income: $50,000

Now let's look at overhead and see how your purchase, design, and operations save you over the course of a year.

Annual supply cost savings, buying from the right vendors, and not oversupplying:

THE POWER OF A LITTLE BIT

You: $900; competition: $1,400

Annual household goods savings, you buying durable goods, and no fluff:

You: $30; Competition: $450

Average appliance and furniture repair and replacement, you making good choices and no bells and whistles, having a good connection with an appliance repair technician and a handyman that can fix furniture:

You: $600; competition: $1000

Landscaping costs: Lower annual cost because of low maintenance design

You: $800; competition: $1,600

Repairs and Maintenance: Lower due to prevention, qualified labor, and local connections

You: $1,300; competition: $1,900

Annual Utilities: Lower due to your Wi-Fi thermostat, Thermal Insulated Curtains, Routine Air Filter maintenance, etc:

You: $1,800; competition: $2,300

Less Refunds due to fewer cleaning errors, better maintenance, and faster customer resolution:

THE POWER OF A LITTLE BIT

You: $1,000; Competition: $1,800

Average Annual Expenses

Competition: $10,450; You: $6,700

Not calculated in this example are property taxes, insurance, and mortgage payments. There are no tricks to these other than shopping around a lot for insurance, fighting the tax assessor if they jack up your bill, and being smart with your financing costs.

Before these expenses, your net is $61,260, and your competition's net is $50,000, with a difference of $11,260. After taking out the itemized expenses above, your profit is $54,560 and your competition is $39,550, for a difference of $15,010.

Now you can see the vast difference between managing your rental with knowledge and proactive intent. Now multiply the spread over a decade, because that is the time horizon you should be thinking about. After one decade, assuming you invested the difference and got a 10% return, that's about $239k more than the competition. After two decades on just this one small property, that's a difference of about $860,000. Now you can see why people who know what they are doing and do it for the long haul blow amateurs out of the water.

By the way, with a gross income of $61,260 in our example, after paying a good management company a 28% commission rate and taking out the expenses listed above, it would come out to $37,407.20, which is just $2,143 less than the average rental. So in this instance, a management company that knows what they are doing is nearly paying for their increase in cost, allowing you to net about the same amount of money that you would if you were doing all the work yourself and were on call 24 hours a day for your rental. It should also be obvious that a management company charging a standard commission and not getting you higher income and lower expenses will absolutely slaughter your return, and you will probably only be profitable in an awesome market.

As we wrap things up, I hope you were able to draw your own conclusion on what is the right move for you and your family as you went through this book.

While this book is not short, it just scratches the surface of all you need to know. I would encourage you to set goals for your journey, whether that be to launch your rental within 60 days of purchase or to set net income targets for the first three years. But beyond these results-oriented goals, set some goals for the controllable inputs into the success formula. Have a goal to have a 100 percent response rate within one hour on Airbnb. Determine that you will adjust rates weekly, and nobody will be more in tune with the local market than you are. If you are just going to be an investor, determine to be a good partner to your manager, getting them what they ask for and adding value to both them and your property.

Whether you manage solo as a super hero, hire a co-host to share responsibilities, or decide to partner with a full-service property management company, you can still either be successful or a huge, embarrassing failure. The success of your enterprise doesn't hinge on that one choice but on the property selection, setup, and operations capability of those running it day to day. This high-stakes gamble hinges on your ability to stake a claim in a nice fishing hole and have the discipline to craft and maintain a quality net there for the long haul.

If you decide to go for it, determine to do it with excellence and purpose. Go to where the fishing is good and create a killer net for long-term results.

327 | YOUR NET DETERMINES YOUR NET